LAW and the
MORAL ORDER

LAW
and the
MORAL
ORDER

W D LAMONT

ABERDEEN
UNIVERSITY
PRESS

First published 1981
Aberdeen University Press
A member of the Pergamon Group
© W D Lamont 1981

British Library Cataloguing in Publication Data

Lamont, William Dawson
Law and the moral order.
1. Ethics
I. Title
170   BJ1012

ISBN 0-08-025742-9
ISBN 0-08-025746-1 flexi

PRINTED IN GREAT BRITAIN
THE UNIVERSITY PRESS
ABERDEEN

Contents

Contents

Preface

The main purpose of this book is to strengthen moral philosophy's links with the living world, so that ordinary thoughtful men and women may find in this philosophical analysis an aid to their understanding of the moral order.

It is in the tradition of the British moral philosophy which covered the second half of the eighteenth and virtually the whole of the nineteenth century when the outstanding contributors—Adam Smith, Hume, Bentham, Mill, Sidgwick and Green—were men of great stature with wide public interests which profoundly affected the content and quality of their philosophical work. Hume, Bentham and Mill, though not academics, helped to mould thinking in the universities; while the academics, Smith, Sidgwick and Green, had a corresponding influence on social and political attitudes. The inevitable effect of this reciprocal influence of public activity and reflective thought was that the detailed pursuit of problems in moral philosophy contributed to the development of some disciplines now known as social sciences. In various universities we can actually trace the process whereby economics, jurisprudence and political theory—to name obvious examples—were gradually carried to the point at which, by the late nineteenth century, they could become autonomous studies. Indeed their acquisition of this independence was partly due to the fact that the fledglings had grown so large and demanding that in some cases the philosophical parents were glad to push them out of the nest.

The withdrawal of such a rich content from moral philosophy in the old comprehensive sense has had some unfortunate consequences. With hindsight we can see that, while the future of ethics (another name for moral philosophy) undoubtedly lay with greater concentration on fundamental principles, the exploration of those principles required to be undertaken in close collaboration with the new social sciences, for only by such association can the moral philosopher deepen his understanding of the nature of the moral order. But, failing to appreciate the new situation, many philosophers assumed that concentration on fundamental principles meant a narrowing of their function to the analysis of abstract moral concepts in isolation from the everyday world in which these concepts had evolved through practical use.

One effect of this withdrawal was that some social studies, notably economics, embraced doctrines which the moralist could have shewn to be theoretically untenable.

On the philosophical side there was a retreat from reality, ethical theory growing ever more narrowly academic, its content determined by changing fashions in logic and theory of knowledge. Thus in the first quarter of the present century a reaction against the Idealism of T H Green in favour of a

Realist theory of knowledge produced G E Moore's *Principia Ethica,* a naive objectivist theory of valuation, the contention being that goodness in the ultimate sense is a quality we simply see to inhere in the thing to which we attribute value. The practical irrelevance of this type of theory becoming apparent, fashion swung to the opposite extreme with an equally naive subjectivist or emotivist doctrine, valuation being regarded as simply an expression of attraction or repulsion. This interpretation proving equally sterile, ethics tended to become identified with the study of value language (as distinguished from substantive value concepts), often in relation to very trivial topics.

It would be quite untrue to suggest that this is a complete picture of contemporary ethics. One can think of individual philosophers who, firmly grounded in the older tradition, refused to be swept away by the currents of changing fashion; and in at least some of the universities there is a refreshing recognition of the fact that ethics must renew and extend its association with other appropriate disciplines if it is to justify its place in the academic world. But even with this qualification we have to admit that the main stream of ethical theorising in this country has ceased to have any serious impact on public attitudes to moral issues.

My purpose, therefore, is to conduct a philosophical analysis which will make more intelligible the nature of the moral order. This is not a realm inhabited by some spiritual élite. It is the workaday world covering family, economic, political, cultural and religious associations, the world in which people try to decide what things are good and bad, what pattern of life it would be sensible and honourable to pursue, how far individuals are responsible for the quality of life in their society, and how far personal and political standards of behaviour can be identical.

It must be understood that moral philosophy does not pretend to deal with these questions on a practical level. Its function is to identify and elucidate the principles in accordance with which answers to practical questions may be sought. While there may be particular fields in which philosophy can make useful contributions, by far the most important task of the philosopher is to elucidate the ultimate standards by reference to which we assess good and evil, right and wrong.

How do we set about this task? Certainly not by trying to define ultimate standards which men 'ought' to adopt. Such an attempt would, indeed, be irrational. Since any 'ought' implies a standard by which it is assessed, an ultimate standard can only be one in accordance with which all 'oughts' are ultimately determined. It cannot itself be meaningfully asserted as a standard that ought to be adopted. If it is ultimate it just *is* adopted. Consequently the task of the moral philosopher is not to promulgate by means of some special insight the principles which ought to rule our lives, but to identify and make explicit those which are implicitly operative in our minds when assessing situations and making decisions. The central problems of ethics are thus factual in the sense that they have to be approached through a systematic study of the ways in which men actually evaluate things, situations and proposed lines of action as good or evil, right or wrong.

In so far as the history of ethics has been positively fruitful, every student of the subject can benefit from acquaintance with the work of his predecessors. But ethical theory has not been invariably fruitful; and so there are two very different questions to be asked as we approach the subject. The first is: what does a direct study of ordinary moral experience shew to be the nature and source of its main concepts and governing principles? The second is: what works in the history of ethics afford positive help in answering this first question? While the second cannot be intelligibly discussed except in association with the first, the first can be treated with little reference to the second; and it is the first of these questions with which we shall be concerned.

Consequently, references to ethical writings, other than the Kantian analysis of moral judgement in Chapter VIII, will be reduced to a minimum. The view here adopted is that any advance in contemporary moral philosophy must depend on making use of work in the social sciences. The social science necessarily associated with an enquiry into our ideas of right and wrong is jurisprudence, the study of positive law. The essential concepts are the same in law and morals, and an acquaintance with the systematic exposition of these concepts in judicial practice and legal theory is essential for a sound understanding of the moral order. It may safely be asserted that a study associating jurisprudence with ethics provides the only standpoint from which we can assess what is living and what is dead in twentieth century ethics.

Acknowledgements

In the present enterprise I have been generously aided by some very good friends. Mr R S Downie, Professor of Moral Philosophy in the University of Glasgow, read and made valuable suggestions on an earlier draft. In dealing with topics in jurisprudence I have been singularly fortunate in enlisting the expert assistance of Mr D N MacCormick, Professor of Jurisprudence in the University of Edinburgh, and Mr R H S Tur, recently Lecturer in Jurisprudence in the University of Glasgow and now Fellow and Tutor of Oriel College, Oxford. They have both read the whole script in two successive drafts and advised on general presentation and inclusion of legal material. Indeed, it might with some justification be said that this is about as near to being a joint work as it could be while remaining under the name of a single author. For its final grooming, anyone familiar with the Aberdeen University Press will appreciate the profit and pleasure I derived from a number of sessions with the publishing director, Mr Colin MacLean. From my wife I have had unfailing encouragement and support in the many ways which only she could give.

W D Lamont

Analytical Table of Contents

the self-conscious volitional level of existence activity is neither merely mechanistic nor merely organic but teleological. It results in the growth of behaviour patterns which, for the individual, are both given and willed. . . . . (11)

(a) The Pattern as *Given*. Folkways may persist over the generations from century to century; and this acceptance of tradition depends initially on the tendency to imitation and assimilation, as exemplified in normal childhood. . . . . (12)

(b) The Pattern as *Willed*. But imitation of behaviour and assimilation of ideas are activities, not passive states, requiring the ability to form general ideas. Ideas of good, bad, right and wrong imply the use of norms which determine what will be accepted or rejected under these ideas. Hence a traditional behaviour pattern can be such only because it is voluntarily conserved and transmitted by successive generations. At any given time and for any given individual it is primary valuational material *given* to him; but it can be so given only because it has been *willed* by past generations. . . . . (12)

2 **Discovery.** This is an authentic material source inasmuch as knowledge of causal relationships relevant to some end within an existing pattern of values can lead to long-term development of the system as a whole. . . . . (13)

3 **Cultural Contact.** As a material source this differs from Discovery in that Discovery, while relevant to existing values, is itself expressed in purely existential judgements, while Cultural Contact brings to bear an alien traditional behaviour pattern to which the indigenous one will be adjusted in so far as modification is considered conducive to a better way of life. . . . . (14)

Chapter 3 *Practical Reason*

Any system of values has a formal structure which has its source in our rational nature. This chapter considers three of the main concepts under which practical reason operates, namely Utility, Economy and Integrity.

1 **Utility.** Utilitarianism is a name applied to theories which define moral right and wrong in terms of some supreme good or goods to be obtained; but Utility is here used in its general sense as indicating a means to an end. It is a valuational, not a causal concept; for if b could be caused by a, a does not have utility unless b is actually desired and a chosen as a means to that end. Utility can refer to either unilateral or reciprocal valuation. . . . . (17)

Unilateral valuation is concerned with the adaptation of means to one specifically envisaged end, while *reciprocal* valuation refers to the ways in which two or more objectives, independently desired, may be means and ends to each other. The concept of Utility, then, applies when two or more ends are instrumentally related, what has utility becoming itself an end with a subordinate place in the valuational system. . . . . (18)

2 **Economy.** Valuation is often complicated by the composite character of either the end to be attained or the means to be used. In either case the concept of Economy becomes operative, the Law of Diminishing Returns necessitating an appeal to the Norm of Marginal Utility. . . . . (19)

(1) The Law of Diminishing Returns is best illustrated by cases in which a unitary end is to be achieved by a co-ordination of complementary means. The efficiency of the enterprise depends on the different means being used in the right proportions because the total end product diminishes relatively to costs when any one factor is increased or diminished out of accord with the optimum combination. . . . . (19)

(2) The Norm of Marginal Utility can best be illustrated by a case in which the end is a complex of parts, each independently produced but all competing for the same limited means. Valuation under the norm of marginal utility is ideally present when the means are so distributed that to subtract any of the

resources from one part of the end and use it for another part would be detrimental to the fulfilment of the end as a whole. We are, of course, talking of an ideal distribution to which a rational being aspires. . . . . (20)

3 Integrity. Economy in the promotion of a complex end is called into play only because the complex is valued as a whole. This points to a third valuational concept most conveniently called Integrity. It is of wide significance, not only for economics in the narrow sense but also for aesthetics and morals. Indeed we may say that the importance of the concepts Utility, Economy and Integrity is the reverse of our order of exposition, since valuation in general is a volitional attitude directed to the creation and preservation of a whole system of values. . . . . (21)

4 'Self-Realisation.' While the aforementioned concepts may suggest that all valuation is directed to some one objective end, simple or complex, and ultimately to a *Summum Bonum*, this suggestion is incompatible with ordinary experience. The individual's life pattern is rendered more or less coherent, not by the vision of an objective end but by an integrating power intrinsic to his nature. What we have called his system of values is better described as a federation of sub-systems, each with a firm nucleus as a condition of effective action, but with open boundaries subjecting it to influence from other sub-systems. . . . . (22)

While the sub-systems are organised under leading concepts, these concepts are but ways in which Practical Reason operates, and it is an attribute of the self as a whole. As the centre from which all valuational activity flows, the member of a moral order is himself the source of his over-all pattern of values. This is what the Idealist philosophers had in mind when they referred (rather misleadingly) to 'self-realisation' as the supreme good. . . . . (23)

Chapter 4 *The Spiritual Attribute of Personality*   25

Having established that the member of a moral order is the source of all values which can be values for him, we come to the second requirement of such an order, namely that he must be the initiator and controller of material events. The first question to be dealt with is the nature of a being capable of constructing a system of values.

1 The Legal and Psychological Conception of Personality. The member of a moral order, as a self-directing centre of intellect and will, is in legal and psychological theory a person; but we shall be concerned with the nature of personality only to elucidate the attribute or attributes which enable him to organise value systems and conform to norms. . . . . (25)

2 The Spiritual Pre-Condition of Knowledge. What is the essential pre-condition of intellectual activity in the knowledge of a world in space and time? Awareness of a series in time implies the operation in the mind of a unifying factor which holds together past, present and future. This attribute of personality cannot be conceived in purely temporal terms, experience of a temporal series implying the operation of a mental attribute transcending the limitations of temporal process. Similarly, experience of a three-dimensional world in space involves a synthesising activity which cannot be described in spatial terms. . . . . (26)

3 Concept of a Spiritual Attribute. Space and time being concepts applicable to the material world, we require some term other than 'material' to describe the attribute of a person in virtue of which he can become aware of such a world. 'Spiritual' would seem to be appropriate, allowing us to speak of 'the spiritual attribute of self-hood' as distinctive of a being who is a self-directing centre of intellectual activity. . . . . (27)

4 The Spiritual Pre-Condition of Volitional Activity. Since at the rational level volitional activity cannot be independent of intellectual activity, the spiritual attribute must be involved in valuation as in knowledge. The argument is not for the existence of a person as a 'spiritual *being*' transcending the limitations of

Chapter 5 *Causality and Teleology*

1 CAUSALITY

Chapter 8 *The Moral Ideal* 55

3 Universality: Supreme Concept of Practical Reason. To say that the moral quality of action consists in respect for the pure form of law (universality) may seem an intellectual abstraction with no practical relevance. Nonetheless, this is the philosophical formulation of the ordinarily accepted criterion of moral goodness—the golden rule. Kant shews this rule ('Do as you would be done by') to have its source in our rational nature by expounding two complementary propositions: (1) 'The good will acts only on maxims it can will as law', and (2) 'The good will always respects persons *as* persons'. . . . . (59)

(1) *The Good Will as Respect for Law* means that the ultimate moral test is that of universalisation—the universalisation of the *maxim* of a proposed action (not, as some mistakenly suppose, universalisation of the proposed action itself), i.e. the willing of the maxim as law. In this connexion, two questions arise: (i) When is it possible and when impossible to universalise a maxim? and (ii) If it cannot be universalised why is its adoption morally wrong? . . . . . (60)

(i) The possibility of universalisation depends on whether the erection of a maxim into a law would or would not involve volitional self-contradiction. A person's planning of his life in accordance with a system of values—popularly called 'the pursuit of personal happiness'—takes for granted a juridical order within which he lives. Any rule which he believes would jeopardise that order *as required by his view of his happiness* could not possibly be willed by him. He could not will both the legal order and a rule of law incompatible with it. Even to attempt such a volitional self-contradiction is impossible for a rational being. . . . . (61)

(ii) As to why it would be morally wrong to adopt a non-universalisable maxim, this is not a question to be answered by the moral theorist. It is a philosophical formulation of the basic contention of the ordinary moral consciousness, the golden rule, which it is the business of the philosopher to elucidate. His contribution is to shew that, the supreme moral concept being that of universality, the golden rule has its source in our rational nature; for the power of apprehending and acting conformably to universals belongs to reason alone. The morally good will is the supreme expression of Practical Reason. This does not mean that one can read off moral conclusions from the abstract formula, or that one should never proceed to act without applying the test of universalisation. It means that if one ever has to appeal to first principles, this is the principle of 'last resort', to which appeal is made. . . . . (63)

(2) *The Good Will as Respect for Personality.* The golden rule says nothing about respect for law. The emphasis is on personal relations; and this is precisely the emphasis in Kant's complementary formula. If we ask 'What *is* law?', the answer is 'A system of universals governing the relations of persons'. A person is a being capable of exercising rights and performing duties; and

Chapter 9 *Community*   67

legislative act which the agent affirms to be valid for men universally. True, this legislative act is merely a means of discovering the agent's own right or duty and is binding on no other person. It is, however, potentially valid for mankind as a whole. . . . . (71)

The potentiality would become an actuality if each member of the community had perfectly infallible knowledge of all relevant facts and future possibilities. As so endowed, with each person affirming maxims as laws, the result would necessarily be a complete consensus of laws willed by all. Each, as willing the laws, would be sovereign in the community, and subject as unconditionally bound to obedience. . . . . (71)

Of course the required omniscience is an impossibility, and the Kingdom-of-Ends can never be an actual state of society. It is an ideal. But not a mere ideal. It is the ideal of a community into which a person must think himself when faced by the need to make a moral judgement. . . . . (72)

How far is this conception of a Kingdom-of-Ends relevant to the making of positive law? In particular, how far can members of a community participate in the making of the law? And how far can performance be assessed by reference to the Kantian ideal? . . . . . (72)

(2) *The Sources of Positive Law and the General Will*. As to general participation in the making of positive law, we note that in most well developed systems the sources are: Judicial Precedent, Authoritative Writings, Equity, Custom and Legislative Enactment. With regard to the first three of these sources, the members of the community in general play no part. . . . . (72)

Custom is best considered in its oldest form as folk-law which evolved in the course of settling disputes at general meetings. As a rule the proceedings were restricted to the older men, women and young men being discouraged from intervening. Decided cases formed precedents, and two factors operated to narrow the range of persons participating. One was the growth of professional juriscolsults who tried to systematise the rules and transmit the product as authoritative tradition. The other factor was the trend in replacing tribal chiefs by royal officers. It is therefore clear that the actual making of the folk-law was not done by the community as a whole. . . . . (73)

But the members of an early community would not, in any case, have wanted to claim participation in making the law. It was ascribed to some divine patron or heroic ancestor, and this imposed a considerable obstacle to arbitrary rule. The position was: on the one hand, the community in general had actually no share in making the law; on the other, it had a degree of control over the lawmakers in virtue of the popularly conceived origin of the system and the consequent withdrawal of authority from rulers who flouted deep-rooted conviction. . . . . (74)

Legislation. The law-making powers of the modern State over its own people are limited only by the extent to which it recognises other independent authorities. With this downgrading of folk law and belief in supernatural sanctions, the ancient safeguards against arbitrary rule vanish, and political institutions are evolved. Two questions: Do legislative institutions increase general participation in the making of law? The answer is No. Are they any substitute for the ancient checks on arbitrary government? It depends on the type of institution. In autocracy the ancient safeguards are lost. In democracy they are enhanced by unfettered, enlightened discussion of public affairs, and by the power to expel legislators who lose public confidence. . . . . (75)

The sovereignty of each member of the Kingdom-of-ends is an essential concept of the moral order. Does it extend to the making of positive law at the political level? No. . . . . (75)

choosing; and so the question is about the nature of voluntary choice. Choice is the overt expression of a valuation; it is directed to producing a state of affairs as an ingredient in an existing system of values in an assessed factual situation. I.e., an act of choice is the response rationally required by a scheme of values and assessed situation. As this is true of all voluntary choice—moral, immoral or non-moral—the libertarian argument cannot be true; for to say there could have been a choice *not* required by the existing values and assessed situation is a self-contradiction, affirming a power of choice which is no choice at all. . . . . (84)

2 Culpability and Voluntary Choice. Moral standards are discerned and authenticated by the individual conscience. It follows that there can be a sense of culpability only if one is already committed to the standard which the present action dishonours. . . . . (85)

But the real conflict is not between a single standard and a single act of choice. It is between two value sub-systems, the one to which the actual choice belongs and the one to which the standard belongs. There is a cleavage within the individual's volitional life. The sense of culpability is awareness of this cleavage and an affirmation of a higher value to the sub-system actually rejected. This paradox is explained by the fact that a person's choice is never made in the light of his total system of values; and when a clash with acknowledged standards becomes apparent, self-identification with the standards (rather than with the actual choice) is the affirmation of unitary selfhood by Practical Reason. . . . . (85)

3 Culpability and the Alternative Choice. While the sense of culpability implies 'I could have chosen otherwise', it does not mean 'in precisely one and the same situation'. '*Ought—can*' is offered as a theoretical, analytic proposition; but 'I could have chosen otherwise' is the expression of a volitional attitude; and with the imperative quality characteristic of all value judgement, it affirms the over-riding goodness of the moral order. It is important to distinguish 'I could have chosen otherwise' (the self-identification in principle with the moral order) from 'I can choose otherwise' (a particular resolve for future behaviour). . . . . (86)

But does not this interpretation of the sense of culpability evade the whole question of liability to punishment for what was actually done? The answer is that punishment (as distinguished from reparation) has nothing to do with *moral* culpability which relates to a personally accepted standard while punishment relates to a standard imposed by an external authority. . . . . (87)

'I can choose otherwise' refers to contemplated future behaviour. It is a complete commital to use all means necessary to success. It is not an exercise of free will in the libertarian sense, but an attitude of resolution plus examination of existing values and adjustment of external circumstances to ensure that the required choice will conform to the ideal. . . . . (88)

4 Personal Autonomy. Responsibility is primarily answerability, moral responsibility being answerability to the moral order for the fulfilment of one's obligations as a member. Two questions arise: First, what are the demands of membership? Essentially, respect for the personality of others as actual situations arise. Second, how is it possible to fulfil the obligations? The ability is an intrinsic attribute of rational nature. But this applies equally to transgression, for only a rational being can be and feel culpable. There are degrees of rational behaviour, depending on the concepts—Utility, Economy, Integrity and Universality—in accordance with which choices are made. In a moral context culpability arises when the concept of Universality has been inoperative. . . . . (89)

Culpability is ascribed, not to a part of one's volitional activity, not merely to the sub-system of values requiring the immoral choice but to the volitional attitude as a whole, since the aspiration to conformity has not overcome the

with the nature of responsibility itself but with objective circumstances in which responsible choice has to take place. As to Necessity or Coercion, the moral philosopher is concerned only to note the responses to crimes committed under these conditions; and the trend appears to be an acceptance of diminished culpability, especially when the threat is to life or limb as distinguished from property. . . . . (99)

But the question of crime committed under superior orders has greater moral significance. Originating in a conflict of legal duties, it is specially concerned with immunities. The most obvious case is where orders are operative within a system such as a military organisation. There, immunity is greatest at the lowest level and criminal liability increases as we ascend the heirarchy of command. For this reason acts of State are supremely open to scrutiny at the bar of justice, since that is the level at which the moral order is best maintained. But in actual practice, decisions in this area seem to be influenced as much by expediency and general principles as by rules of law. . . . . (100)

II Punishment
To whom is punishment applied? What is its apparent aim?

1 Liability to Punishment. Of the four possible states of mind associated with the commission of a wrong, Innocent Mistake and Negligence do not shew actual disrespect for the law, while Recklessness and Deliberate Intent do. These latter two states of mind, by almost universal practice, carry liability to punishment. Negligence is not always distinguishable from Recklessness, but when the distinction is clear, it, like Innocent Mistake, is in principle immune. Many qualifications to this generalisation would be necessary in any work on jurisprudence; but the general principle is that penalties are properly imposed only so far as prior awareness of illegal consequences does not deter from a proposed action. . . . . (102)

2 Aim of Punishment

(1) *Retribution* (from *re-tribuere*) means generally to give or assign, but is now used exclusively in the sense of inflicting a penalty. At the most simple level of spontaneous retaliation it has no aim since it is not a voluntary action. . . . . (103)

Practised under the conception of *lex talionis* it is voluntary and therefore purposive, the objective being a balancing-down to make the penalty a replica of the crime. At this stage there is no distinction drawn between physical act (*actus reus*) and mental attitude (*mens rea*), or between reparation and punishment. But the first of these distinctions is implicit when different penalties are assigned to killing on sudden encounter and killing by way of ambush, the penalties being directed to different attitudes of will. As so directed the penalties are clearly intended to influence the will which can refer only to future behaviour and hence intended as deterrent. . . . . (103)

(2) *Deterrence.* To regard deterrence as the sole aim of punishment, other than the aim of levelling-down under the *lex talionis,* is to adopt a utilitarian interpretation. The threat of a penalty is an appeal to reason, a challenge to take it into account as part of the assessed situation which, along with the person's system of values, will determine the required future choice. . . . . .

The threat of penalties is thus comparable to the aids a person adopts to overcome some temptation. In the one case, the agent himself adjusts the situation which (he hopes) will require a choice other than surrender to the temptation. In the other case, the aids (threatened penalties) are provided by an outside authority. . . . . (104)

But just as the aids adopted by a person can be permanently effective only

Introduction

The moral order is a normative order. That is to say, it consists of a community of persons pursuing their individual and collective ways of life, and adjusting particular objectives and policies according to certain rules, standards or norms of behaviour. Most people, if not all, assume that there is a supreme standard called the 'moral ideal' or 'moral law' or 'Will of God', the description depending on individual background of belief. Whether this assumption can be rationally justified is one of the major questions to be discussed in what follows; but for the present it is sufficient to observe that at least some standards are essential for the life of any community.

Potentially, the moral order embraces humanity at large, but it actually exists only to the extent that men live in communities. In a well developed political society there is a complex of normative systems including (to name but the most obvious ones) the positive law of the State; generally recognised social customs; professional codes such as medical and legal ethics; religious institutions in so far as they endeavour to direct conduct; and the ideals of the individual members.

Of the members of a moral order two propositions must be true.

1 The values attached by the individual to things and activities can be determined only by himself. What is actually, objectively good *for* him in a given situation may be apparent to others and not to him. But what can be conceived as good *by* him is necessarily determined by his own assessment of that situation, his reading of the facts and his interpretation of the norms to which he gives allegiance. In short, the individual, as a centre of intellect and will, is the source of all values which can be conceived as values by him.

2 Since a person, in pursuit of what he conceives to be good, is an active agent in the material world, it follows that he is an initiator, director and controller of events in that world.

These two propositions which indicate the foundations of a moral order have been implicitly or explicitly challenged. The first is opposed by the religious contention that what is good is revealed by divine command, or by a philosophical doctrine which asserts value to be intrinsic to the thing valued. The second proposition is opposed by the view that everything which happens in the world, including the voluntary behaviour of rational beings, is explicable in terms of causal necessity.

Since acceptance of either of these positions would deny the existence of a moral order, Part One of this book will be concerned with a survey of the foundations of such an order. Chapters 1–3 will explain the nature of valuation, shewing that all values have their source in the creative activity of rational beings, while Chapters 4–5 will deal with the nature of voluntary conduct as explicable in terms of teleology, not of causality.

Part Two, on Positive Law and the Moral Ideal, will deal with the structure of the moral order itself. While, as already explained, the moral order embraces a complex of norms, I shall concentrate on two particular normative systems, namely positive law and the moral ideal as revealed in the individual conscience. These are chosen because positive law is the area in which the basic concepts of a normative order have been most systematically expounded, and it is in the individual conscience that we have the ultimate assessments of right and wrong.

The prominence thus given to a discussion of positive law in a book on moral philosophy is admittedly unusual. The justification is that such a partnership of jurisprudence and ethics should encourage philosophers to keep in touch with real moral issues, often forgotten amid the pleasures of academic debate.

Part Three, on Corrective Justice, will cover the ethical aspects of Reparation, Responsibility, and Crime and Punishment.

Foundations of the Moral Order

CHAPTER ONE

The Conative Basis of Valuation

1. THE NOTION OF INTRINSIC GOODNESS

It is sometimes held that value or goodness in the ultimate sense is an intrinsic property or quality of the thing or action to which it is being attributed. The attraction of this view is readily understood. Since there is much controversy over the values advocated and promoted by individuals and groups, there must be some test by which they can be assessed. Valuations or value judgements are either true or false, and there must be some way of discovering which are true and which false.

Since many of our valuations are merely relative, goodness being attributed to a thing only as a means to some ulterior end, and therefore implying the goodness of the end, it may be supposed that all values are derived ultimately from some thing or things which are good not merely relatively but absolutely. Goodness, the argument then runs, must be in the last analysis an objective property or quality inherent in, intrinsic to, the nature of the thing or action to which the goodness is being attributed.

But the belief in intrinsic goodness is found, on examination, to be nothing more than an expression of subjective, arbitrary preference. This becomes clear if we ask 'What is intrinsically good?'. One answer is 'pleasure', another 'virtue and knowledge', and still another 'aesthetic experience'. If we further ask, 'How do you know these things to be intrinsically good?', we are apt to be told 'It is self-evident', which is just another way of saying 'I am convinced that they are'. And the basis of this conviction? The answer of G E Moore[1] is illuminating. He had committed himself to an extreme form of the intrinsic theory. Goodness, he held, is inherent in the thing taken by itself, out of all relation to anything else. Hence, if I want to know whether a thing has this quality, I ask myself 'Suppose that it existed absolutely alone—constituting, as it were, the whole universe—would I prefer its existence to its non-existence?'. If I would, then it is intrinsically good. In other words, intrinsic goodness is a term to describe anything we happen to want taken out of every context in which it is experienced. This is extreme objectivism turned outside-in to produce extreme subjectivism.

It may be suggested that the trouble here is not in the notion of intrinsic goodness but in the argument, or lack of it, brought in defence of the idea. But the position is much more serious. The idea is inherently indefensible.

Suppose we start with a proposition that is unlikely to be challenged by anyone who has seriously reflected on the matter, the proposition, namely, that the attribution of goodness includes a provisional urge or encouragement to create or maintain the thing of which the goodness is asserted. The meaning of 'good', that is to say, includes a *prima facie* imperative that the thing be brought into or maintained in existence. The meaning of 'bad' includes the *prima facie* imperative that it should not exist. The demand or imperative is only provisional or *prima facie* because circumstances may indicate a higher priority for other measures. The point is that there is at least the provisional imperative included in the meaning. This is why it is supposed that, by postulating an objective existence for goodness we have a firm foundation for our system of values.

Since the demand is part of the meaning of the concept, then to say that goodness is an objective quality of the thing in question means that the demand comes from that thing itself. The thing or action demands—literally demands—'Realise (or maintain) me!'. This is sheer nonsense. No thing or act can issue a demand since this can come only from a being possessed of intellect and will.

Shall we say, then, that the goodness is intrinsic to the thing, but that the imperative issues from an intelligent being? On this assumption, goodness is simply a property or quality of the thing like any other property or quality included in its factual description. No statement about the factual nature of a thing ever carries an imperative, or even a suggestion for action. If I say, 'Racial discrimination is a characteristic of South African law', this carries no hint whatsoever as to whether this characteristic should be encouraged or condemned. But the imperative can never be removed from the meaning of goodness or badness. While goodness cannot be an intrinsic quality of the thing to which it is attributed, the imperative aspect is intrinsic to the attribution of goodness. If I say 'It is bad that a legal system should provide for racial discrimination', it would be incompatible with this valuation to encourage the practice and wholly compatible to work for its discontinuance.

Since it is evident (i) that no list of qualities included in a merely factual description ever carries an imperative, and (ii) that the ascription of goodness or badness always carries a *prima facie* imperative, then goodness cannot be a property or quality of the thing of which it is asserted. (To reply, as some do, that goodness is a non-natural quality takes us nowhere. It merely says that goodness is not a quality in any sense in which the term is naturally used.)

It is also evident that, since the meaning of goodness does carry an imperative content, and since an imperative can come only from the will or volitional attitude of a rational being, the ascription of goodness must be itself a *prima facie* imperative with its source in the volitional nature of a rational being, human or divine.

Actually, the distinction between human and divine will is irrelevant in the present context. The imperative content of the idea of goodness can exist only for the person who in a given situation acknowledges some thing or action to be good. Whatever imperatives may issue from Mount Sinai, if a son of Jacob does not think it would be good to obey, then for him in that situation there can be no imperative included in the idea of the goodness of obeying, for the simple reason that he is not attributing goodness to obedience in this particular case. He recognises an imperative issuing from Sinai, all right; but an *imperative included in the concept of goodness* can exist only for someone who is actually attributing goodness to some thing or action.

It is therefore manifest that the imperative is part of the individual's own act of valuation; and an act of valuation, because it contains a *prima facie* imperative, is primarily a volitional activity.

2. VALUATION A CONATIVE ATTITUDE

Valuation is primarily a volitional attitude. It is also a judgement, and a judgement is true or false. But how can a volitional attitude be true or false? We shall deal with the question in two stages, shewing first the essentially conative character of valuation.

People assess things, states of affairs and actions as good or bad, desirable or undesirable, right or wrong; and these assessments are called valuations or value judgements, as distinguished from existential judgements which indicate factual situations (as for example, 'The cat is on the mat' or 'Buckingham Palace is in London'). The first pair of terms, 'good' and 'bad', are the most comprehensive in the sense that they can be used to express valuations in general. As the Oxford English Dictionary has it, 'good' is a term of general or indeterminate commendation, and 'bad' has generally the contrary sense. Thus, 'It is desirable that the old age pension be increased' can be restated as 'It would be good if the old age pension were increased'; and for 'It is wrong to punish the innocent' we can substitute 'It is bad to punish the innocent'. Of course the reduction of a value judgement to these general terms omits its specific character and therefore the context in which its truth can be measured. But we are here concerned with the general character of all valuation, and so the specific character of different types can be ignored.

All valuational terms, general and specific, occur in opposed pairs—good, bad; better, worse; desirable, undesirable; right, wrong; beautiful, ugly; prudent, extravagant; useful, worthless; and so forth. This linkage of contradictory terms which challenge each other with reference to the same thing or action distinguishes valuation from existential judgement, a distinction to be borne in mind when the same word can be used in different senses. If one says, 'The owner of the orchard gave the young thief a good hiding', would it make sense to say, 'No, it was a bad hiding'? If so, 'good' has been used in a valuational sense. But if it only means 'severe', as it usually does, the narrator of the incident probably spoke with approval while the culprit might conceivably use the same description but hardly with approval. Again, if I say 'That is my good brother over there', I am probably not contrasting him with my bad brother but merely indicating the presence of my brother-in-law.

Valuation operates with the linked contraries 'good' and 'bad' because it is not concerned with the factual description of things or actions but with a *pro* or *con* attitude to them. It is a potential or actual commitment; and the difference between an existential and a value judgement becomes obvious if we compare the relation between existential judgement and overt choice, on the one hand, with the relation between value judgement and overt choice, on the other. It will be convenient to return to our previous example. Take the existential judgement (i) 'South African law discriminates against coloured people'. Having assented to this, it would not be incompatible for me to say (a) 'I support the introduction of a similar policy for Great Britain.' Neither would there be anything contradictory of the existential judgement if I said (b) 'I resolutely oppose any adoption of that policy in Great Britain'. The practical attitudes (a) and (b) are in direct conflict with each other, but neither is in conflict with the judgement (i), for it is a mere statement of fact without any implications for the practical attitude of the speaker. But if I make the value judgement (ii) 'It is utterly bad to discriminate against coloured people', it would be completely incompatible to express the practical attitude (a) and wholly compatible, and indeed reinforcing, to express the attitude (b). And since the value judgement (ii) can oppose one practical attitude and support its contrary, it must itself be essentially the expression of a practical attitude, not a mere statement of fact.

The distinction between existential and value judgement can be put in more technical terms. Psychologists are generally agreed that every mental state has three aspects: cognitive, conative and affective (or emotive); but that, while all three are ever present, one or other aspect is generally dominant, giving its character to the mental state as a whole. Thus, we should regard perceiving, believing, understanding and inferring as *cognitive* attitudes; desiring, willing and advocating as *conative*; and being pleased, pained, fearful or joyful as *affective* or *emotive* attitudes. An existential judgement is primarily cognitive, expressing what is perceived, etc., while a value judgement is primarily conative. Thus, to attribute goodness to a certain state of affairs is to express a conative attitude towards its maintenance or production. In other words, an existential judgement is *informative about* the objective order, while a value judgement is *potentially formative of* the objective order.

It should be observed that we speak of valuation as *potentially* formative of the objective order. It is not the same as overt choice, for there are many things which we call good without taking any steps to bring them about. A person may strongly disapprove of seeing someone discard litter on the street, know that it is illegal, and yet do nothing to bring the culprit to book. His valuation expresses an 'anti-' attitude; but any conative tendency is liable to be held in check by some other volitional trend and so fail to inspire overt action.

This brings us to the question as to how a primarily conative attitude can be expressed as a true or false judgement.

3. VALUATION AS SYSTEMATISING ACTIVITY
Valuation is the expression of a conative attitude, of approval or disapproval of some thing, state of affairs or action. But while every valuation is an expression of approval-or-disapproval, the converse does not hold. To ascribe value is to

express approval, but the expression of approval is not necessarily the ascription of value. Approval is an inner subjective attitude while valuation is an assertion about the object or action to which the attitude is directed. To say 'I like smoking' expresses a subjective attitude; but to say 'Smoking is good(bad)' is to evaluate the practice. It may well be that a state of 'mere subjective approval' which does not involve any element of valuation is only a limiting concept, and that it would be impossible for a rational being to approve of some object without implicitly asserting something about it; but in so far as one can approach to this limit, to that extent we have the mere subjective state of approval and not a value judgement.

But whether or not there can be approval without valuation, our interest is in valuation. Suppose that I like drinking at the village inn; this is an activity of which, by the simple fact of indulging in it, I express approval. But I may evaluate the activity in either of two ways. I may say 'Drinking at the inn is a good habit to be cultivated, for it promotes the sense of community'. Or I may say 'It is a bad practice, for the addiction to alcohol is the cause of great social evil'. The evaluation of the habit is also an expression of approval or disapproval, but it is something more. What is the something more?

As this example suggests, valuation is the approval or disapproval of a thing or action in relation to a wider set of approved ends or actions. It is approved as good when it advances or sustains those ends or actions, and it is disapproved as bad when it is incompatible with the wider system.

The activity of valuation is particularly well exemplified in the ancient Hebrew sage's commendation of Wisdom:[2]

> O happy is the man who hears
>   instruction's warning voice,
> And who celestial Wisdom makes
>   his early, only choice.
>
> For she has treasures greater far
>   than east or west unfold;
> And her rewards more precious are
>   than all their stores of gold.
>
> In her right hand she holds to view
>   a length of happy days;
> Riches with splendid honours joined
>   are what her left displays.
>
> She guides the young with innocence
>   in pleasure's path to tread;
> A crown of glory she bestows
>   upon the hoary head.

According as her labours rise,
so her rewards increase;
Her ways are ways of pleasantness
and all her paths are peace.

These fruits of Wisdom—as Mark Twain said of his reported demise—may be somewhat exaggerated, but there can be no doubt as to the nature of the act of valuation itself. Wisdom, we are being told, reveals its goodness, its superlative value, in conducing to a long and happy life, riches, honour, innocent enjoyment in youth and tranquility in revered old age. You display its goodness by exhibiting it in its relations with other things already valued.

But valuation is not merely a relational activity. It is systematically constructive. When the Hebrew sage demonstrates the goodness of wisdom by relating it to riches, honour, etc., he is not affirming those relations as actually existing. Indeed, they cannot all exist at one and the same time (e.g. innocent youth and revered old age). But they have, he assures us, a potential existence; and the potentiality will be translated, as situations develop, into actuality by pursuit of the objective (wisdom) whose value is now being asserted. That is to say, valuation is a volitional attitude directed to the creation and conservation of a pattern of objectives through pursuit of a further objective which thus becomes itself a constituent of the general scheme.

Hence the truth or falsity of a valuation is measured by the extent to which the particular end or objective, now asserted to be good, will or will not consolidate and enrich the pattern of ends in question. Mere approval is neither true nor false, but 'the expressed approval of something as consolidating a pattern of ends' is true or false and subject to an empirical test. Of course to apply the test we must be clear as to whose pattern is in question. Is the person expressing a value with respect to his own narrow interests, those of his family, or his community, or humanity at large? This being understood, the test is the same in principle whatever pattern is contemplated.

The praise of wisdom shews valuation to be concerned with conformity to norms as well as with the co-ordination of ends. Wisdom not only promotes riches and honour but also aids the enjoyment of *innocent* pleasure. It covers both norm-conformity and ends-coherence. Norms, as rules or sets of rules, are instrumental to the achievement of general policies; and particular ends, even general policies, are partly determined by respect for norms.

Valuation is further complicated by the fact that the pattern of ends pursued by the individual does not remain exactly the same throughout his life. The changes may be only consequential on maturing experience, but they may be much more radical. The pursuit of a major interest may evolve in such a way that success in the enterprise will gradually transform the whole mode of life. The small-time grocer, full of ambition to make a success of the business, prospers so well that he opens an increasing number of branches, then acquires control of supplying agencies, buys out his competitors one after another, ending with a commercial empire of which the original grocery is but an insignificant part. He cannot escape the movement into a new social order, and he may finally become best known to the general public as a patron of the arts rather than as a business magnate. In short, there is no set of norms or ends which can be assumed to be the permanent framework of a person's system of values. Conformity to norms and systematising of ends are essential character-istics of valuation; but the modes in which these characteristics manifest themselves are infinitely variable in both individual and group life.

4. INDIVIDUAL CENTRES OF VALUATION

There is a further fact which would seem to ensure that the world of values must always remain in a state of instability. It is the fact that values are created and sustained only in the minds of individual persons. This applies not only to the individual's own pattern of life but also to the value systems of social groups, however large or small. By the very nature of valuation, it can exist only in the mind of the individual. The norms which guide his conduct are neces-sarily only those which, on some ground or other, are acceptable to him; and the systematising activity which creates a pattern of ends is possible only within a unitary self-consciousness.

As we have just said, this essentially personal character of valuation would seem to work for permanent instability or even chaos. But the reality is far otherwise. Changes, tensions and confusions do exist; but what is much more obvious is the stability which is the general condition of the social order. We are therefore faced by the question: How can a world of values created and sustained by individual wills manifest itself as a set of social values binding individuals into a single community?

The first point to make in reply to this question is to indicate an important implication of the fact just noted, namely that the individual's system of values has its source in himself. By nature he belongs to the human race, and this determines the bounds within which his wants will develop. Further, the human race exists only in the form of communities large and small. The individual owes his very existence to parents, and during his early years he is absolutely dependent for survival on some social group. With increasing years he consciously identifies with this group or, in the most extreme form of rejec-tion, its repudiation is the negative aspect of a vision (prophetic or illusory) of a social order nearer to the heart's desire. But in whatever community he elects to live, there will be rules to promote the common good. His acceptance of them will be a condition of membership, and they determine very largely the content of his own system of values. It is not suggested that promotion of the common good is regarded wholly or even mainly as a matter of duty. There is 'a natural inclination to society' born and bred in the individual and this plays its part in the construction of his system of values from the very beginning.

It will be observed that even this skeletal answer to the question 'How can values having their source in the mind of the individual be manifest as a set of social values binding individuals into a single community?' has got to be framed largely in terms of the nature of the moral order, the subject of our Part Two. But there is still a good deal of ground to be covered with respect to the foundations of that order. On the nature of valuation in general there are two quite elementary matters to be considered: we have to look, first, at the sources from which the individual derives the initial material with which he builds up his pattern of values, and this will be the subject of Chapter 2; and, secondly, we have to consider the ways in which this content is given form, the subject of Chapter Three.

CHAPTER TWO
Material Sources

Without attempting a definitive account of the initial contents of our value systems, we shall deal with the three most important sources, namely Traditional Behaviour Patterns, Discovery and Cultural Contact.

1. TRADITIONAL BEHAVIOUR PATTERNS

We must at the outset distinguish between traditional behaviour patterns and the natural conditions under which they are developed, namely the physical environment and man's own biological and psychological nature. These natural conditions set limits to the kind of values a person can entertain. Thus, even within the comparatively small area of the British Isles, early local cultures (e.g. from the sixth to the eighth century AD) obviously reflect geographical differences. The social institutions of the richer Lowlands were geared to a primarily agricultural economy, those of the hill country to a primarily pastoral one.

But while environment and basic human nature set the limits, they do not determine the content of a system of values. Certainly man, like every other constituent member of the universe, maintains his existence by a process of mutual adjustment as between himself and his environment. But there are different levels at which this adjustment takes place. For inorganic nature it is merely mechanistic. For organic nature it involves highly complex internal adjustment to external stimuli. At the selfconscious or rational level it takes on a new character which is neither mechanistic nor merely organic but purposive or teleological. That is to say, it transcends the level of physiological response and is governed by purposes and ideals. This does not mean that we cease to be subject to the laws of nature and organic process, but it does mean that in our specifically rational activities we do not simply react to external events but act in accordance with the conception of an objective order to which we (truly or falsely) believe those events to belong. While basic behaviour patterns fall within limits set by nature, they are themselves the creations of rational beings.

These behaviour patterns have to be viewed from two sides. First, when we speak of them as a traditional material source we imply that their content does not originate with the individual but is *given* to him. But, secondly, when we speak of them as providing the basic material of his system of values we imply that the content is positively *willed*, taken over by him and incorporated into a system. There is no necessary opposition between 'given' and 'willed' content. The terms indicate different stages in the assimilation of a traditional behaviour pattern.

(a) The Pattern as *Given*

Folkways may continue from generation to generation with no apparent reason other than that 'this is the way in which the thing has always been done', and the vitality of tradition is almost incredible. Thus we distinguish whole millennia by differences in the funereal practices, monuments and artefacts of primitive peoples: the long barrow of Neolithic man, the round tumulus and megalithic circle of the Bronze Age, the characteristic fortification of the Iron Age. Indeed the very names Stone, Bronze and Iron refer to traditional types of tool and weapon.

Even in early historic times when literacy has become sufficiently advanced to leave intelligible records, the duration of customary styles is measured in centuries, the mediaeval farmer following exactly the same routine as his forebears. Customary law is intimately bound up with the cultivation of the soil; and even the popular recreations are rooted in pagan or Christian festivals which were originally invocations or thanksgiving for prosperity in seedtime and harvest.

This acceptance of tradition depends initially on the compulsive tendency to imitation and assimilation, best exemplified in the child mind. The individual is born into a society in which a more or less well integrated system of values already exists. He cannot choose between this and some other system, for he cannot conceive of any other. That X is good or bad and Y right or wrong is not, in the earlier stages, a matter of intuition or decision but of information. The child knows that stealing is wrong in the same way as he knows that the man who comes home in the evening and sits at the head of the table is his father; he has been told that it is so. He wears the customary clothes of his time and place because that is what being clothed *is*. He follows the recognised practices in the current games because that is what play *is*. It is on this primarily imitative and assimilative nature of the child mind that Plato based his whole system of kindergarten and primary education.

But Plato had grasped only one half of the truth.

(b) The Pattern as *Willed*

His intention was to stamp a set of values so firmly on the mind in its most formative years that the impression could never be blurred or erased. This presupposed that, in the imitation of actions and assimilation of ideas, children are but passive recipients, that standards and ideas externally created can just be implanted in the mind. To some extent this can actually be achieved by 'brain washing' techniques. But unless they produce a degree of insanity these techniques do not have the desired long-term effect when the victim is let loose to make his way in the real world; and Plato's purpose was to train an elite for leadership in the real world, an essential part of the training being in fidelity to moral standards. What he omitted to take into account is that, by the time explicit consciousness of an objective order has supervened upon instinctive behaviour, imitation is an active process, not a passive submission to the branding-iron. It is the following of a model of a designated character, and it presupposes in the pupil the ability to form general ideas. This ability is also presupposed in the assimilation of even the most elementary conceptions of right and wrong; and the formation of such ideas is an actively discriminating process. It is necessarily discriminative and selective since indiscriminate absorption is incompatible with the classification of actions under general ideas. Once a general idea acquires meaning as a normative concept it acts as a kind of filter through which alleged right and wrong actions must pass before they can be accepted as such. With time and advancing maturity there is developed a critical stance; and the more a person endeavours to live up to the requirements of commonly accepted values, the greater is the likelihood that he will on occasion turn those standards against some of the detail in the traditional behaviour pattern as a whole.

For the present, however, we are concerned, not with attempts to modify the pattern but with its reception, conservation and transmission. Its reception depends on the actively imitative and assimilative powers of the mind. Conservation and transmission are a different matter. Conservation, and hence transmission, depend on a tradition's being not merely received but positively willed. It must be sustained by the wills of the adult community. Their wills are expressed positively in the day-to-day decisions conformable to use and wont, and negatively in resistance to suggested change. Every scientific improver knows how difficult it can be to persuade cultivators in communities with a low level of literacy to adopt more efficient practices; and this is because the old ways are valued (perhaps rightly valued) in the context of a whole culture, and so positively chosen in preference to others.

It is, however, true that even the most conservative behaviour pattern evolves in complex ways. On the foundations of our elemental needs—food, shelter, propagation of the species—a culture is erected which brings a new quality to their satisfaction. The meal becomes a ceremonial occasion for the enhancement of which the skills of craftsmen and artists are brought into play; the rude shelter acquires, over the ages, architectural grace; sexual pairing evolves into family and tribal organisation; and integral to the whole movement is an intellectual probing into the mysteries of the universe. But at any given time the culture constitutes a consolidated tradition which supplies the primary material for the individual's system of values. To him it is 'given', but it can be given to him only because it has been 'willed' by his ancestors and evolved from beliefs and aspirations reaching back into the far unrecorded past.

2. DISCOVERY
Discovery is an authentic material source for any system of values. True, it has to be relevant to some end within an existing system and ultimately to the traditional behaviour pattern which has been assimilated. But within the context of such a system, discovery of hitherto unknown facts may make an important contribution, the long-term effect of which is the continuous development of the system itself.

Thus, despite the largely unvarying routine which was characteristic of mediaeval husbandry, peoples' minds were not impervious to suggestions of change. Such a suggestion came when someone—probably by the merest accident—found that the seed-corn he had received from a neighour produced a noticeably good yield. This suggested a superiority in the neighbour's grain. But using some of the crop for the following year's seed did not have the same satisfactory result. In course of time it became evident that the better yield had something to do with the fact that the seed had been grown on other soil. This was later generalised in Walter of Henley's *Treatise on Husbandry*: 'Seed grown on other ground will bring more profit than that which is grown on your own. Plough two selions at the same time, and sow one with seed which is bought and the other with corn which you have grown; in August you will see that I speak truly'.[3] There would be no unwillingness to test this proposition. It did not recommend anything opposed to the social code. Corn was often bought or borrowed; seed was in many cases given to tenants. Indeed, the recommendation was only proposing as a settled policy what had already been found to work in a significant number of cases.

Nonetheless, the very formulation of the rule and its adoption would be part of a chain reaction. It drew attention to a very odd fact. Why should seed-corn not take kindly to the soil in which it had been nurtured? Was it perhaps just one item in a whole complex of natural phenomena? The question would invite and receive attention on monastic farms and on the demesne lands of enlightened lords rich enough to risk experimentation. It would be noted that there is an apparent analogy in the breeding of stock; and the gradual accumulation of knowledge would eventually produce the kind of agricultural and animal husbandry taught in our contemporary colleges, a system which is itself anything but final.

3. CULTURAL CONTACT

Some communities, by their own initiative, creative imagination and technical skills, have risen from primitive levels to highly developed forms of cultural life. For most, however, cultural contact has been a powerful influence. It differs from 'discovery' in at least one essential respect. Discovery is an intellectual apprehension of fact, the apprehension being expressed in existential judgements. It is a discovery that coal will burn; but this fact has no valuational significance except in the context of the desires for warmth, light and cooking. An alien culture, on the other hand, is like a traditional behaviour pattern in that it is itself a more or less coherent valuational system. The valuational significance of discovery presupposes your existing system, while an alien culture challenges it at various points.

It must be very seldom, if ever, that an immigrant culture, however impressive, wholly supersedes an indigenous one. For western Christendom the principal external influences came from Greece and Rome, and through them from Palestine and Egypt; and in modern times European culture has dominated the world. But in neither case has a new cultural form entirely superseded an old. Rather, the immigrant culture has penetrated and modified the indigenous one to a greater or less degree; and the degree to which an alien culture can be thus assimilated depends on the extent to which it is generally accepted as conducive to a better way of life. That the community life is indeed enriched by such acceptance may often be open to doubt, but that is a matter for long-term practical evaluation. Here we are concerned only with the nature of the process by which cultural assimilation takes place, the point being that it is through a general acceptance of the novel ideas and practices as potentially enriching the main pattern of life already cherished.

The impact of ancient classical and modern European cultures illustrates the one-way influence of higher on lower. When communities are at approximately the same level of development and enjoying continuous intercourse, the influence will be reciprocal, this being clearly so among the industrialised nations of today.

CHAPTER THREE

Practical Reason

In the preceding chapter we have been looking at the material content of a person's system of values in so far as it derives from external sources. But it is a system only in so far as it has form and structure, and these characteristics derive from the active powers of the individual valuer himself. A full description of those powers would have to take account of his nature as a whole, but we are concerned only with those which relate to his ability to make value judgements and pursue what he takes to be good. Valuation, the approval of something as a constituent of a group of ends and norms, involves both the power of visualising potential objectives and also knowing the causal processes which can transform the potential into the actual. Such a power belongs only to a rational being; and so the form and structure of a system of values has its source in our rational nature—in Reason as practically operative, Practical Reason.

How Reason operates in practical affairs cannot be deduced from the concept of Reason itself. As we can present an intelligible account of its theoretical use only by devising a set of logical concepts to describe the ways in which we actually think and communicate and argue, so Reason in its practical use can be described only through concepts relevant to the ways in which valuation takes place.

Here we shall expound its operations in terms of three concepts applicable to valuation in general, omitting for the present any reference to specifically interpersonal relations which fall to be considered in Part Two. The three concepts are Utility, Economy and Integrity.

1. UTILITY

Two points should, perhaps, be made with regard to the term Utility. First, Utility has become closely associated with a particular philosophical school, the Hedonistic Utilitarianism of Bentham and Mill. The name Utilitarianism also covers the theories of G E Moore and Hastings Rashdall,[4] all these thinkers identifying the morally right action with the action which has utility, or is useful as a means to some general end—Pleasure, Happiness, Knowledge, Aesthetic experience having their champions. As used in the present context the term does not refer to any of these schools. It is taken in its strict and proper sense. A thing or action has utility in so far as it is useful as means to a given end.

Second, utility as a means-end relationship should not be confused with the causal (cause-effect) relationship. Suppose that I wish to call on a neighbour, and ring his door-bell to advertise my presence. Operating the bell-push is the initial event in a causal process which ultimately brings my friend to the door.

But my pressing the bell (means) in order to bring him to the door (end) is a purposive activity. It is a cause with respect to the chain of natural events which follow, but a means only because I desire admission (the end). A cause does not, as such, have utility. It has utility only when initiated as a means to an envisaged end; and the adoption of means to end is possible only for a rational being.

That Utility is a concept descriptive of an activity of Reason will be clear if we note the kind of maxims associated with it, such as; 'Whoso wills an end necessarily wills also the known indispensible means'. If a person desires the ability to navigate a vessel across the Atlantic but does not know how to acquire the ability, its attainment is merely a *desired* end. If he does know how to acquire it (e.g. by attending a navigation school) but is unable or unwilling to adopt the means, the attaining of the ability is still merely a desired end. For it to become a *willed* end the known means must be adopted; for willing an end and willing the means are two aspects of the one rational activity.

The concept of Utility can refer to at least two different relationships giving rise, on the one hand, to unilateral valuations and, on the other, to reciprocal valuation.

(1) Unilateral Valuation. This is concerned with the adaptation of means to one specifically envisaged end. The objective may be as simple as sewing a button on a shirt. It may require years of preparation and vast expenditure, as for climbing Everest. It could relate to a comprehensive political objective, a notable example being J C Smuts' vision of an Anglo-Africaans State following the end of the South African War.[5] This grand design was to be fulfilled in a country containing, besides the two dominant racial groups, Africans, Coloureds, Indians and Chinese who were all to be utilised or repatriated according to the requirements of the plan. Despite the great differences between the objectives of sewing on a button, climbing Everest and building a political society, they all have this in common that in each case planned action is directed to achieve one definite end.

(2) Reciprocal Valuation. This refers to the way in which two or more objectives, independently desired, may yet be means and ends to each other. A person might wish to secure an academic post. He might also be attracted by the idea of living in Canada. There is no necessary connexion between the two desires; but going to Canada might assist the project of university employment, and securing an appointment there might be the only way of financing the emigration to Canada. Each end would be a means to realisation of the other. Successful reciprocal valuation on the grand scale is found in the colourful career of John Buchan, first Lord Tweedsmuir.[6] Unlike Smuts, he did not seem to have any all-absorbing commitment. Rather, he was remarkable for his versatility, filling a wide variety of roles, mostly with distinction. Novelist, journalist, historian, social aspirant, publisher, administrator of proconsular eminence—these he was concurrently or in turn; and the variety of his interests is no more striking than the ways in which they nourished each other.

The concept of Utility, then, is relevant when two or more ends are seen to be not only compatible but also instrumentally related. Granting that a person approves of A, and that a mode of action B is seen to be conducive to its realisation, if B is not already desired it will become desired for its utility. Or, granting that several ends, independently desired, are seen to be mutually supporting, the direct approval of each will be intensified by the awareness of their being means and ends to each other.

2. ECONOMY

Utility in its narrowest sense refers to the kind of situation in which a single means will be instrumental in producing a single end. This is so even when, as in 'reciprocal utility', a number of objectives are means and ends to each other: the utility of A is its usefulness in the production of B, and the utility of B is its usefulness in the production of A.

But the fact of reciprocal utility reminds us that life is not a series of unrelated means-end situations. Valuation is often—perhaps generally—confronted by practical problems where there is a composite character in the means to be used or in the end to be achieved. In either case valuation is governed by the concept of Economy which limits the extent to which simple utility will affect decisions.

In their theory of valuation under the concept of Economy economists have used two illuminating subordinate concepts, namely 'the law of diminishing returns' and 'the norm of marginal utility', employed in the analysis of industrial, commercial and administrative affairs. We shall use them just in so far as they help to explain the nature of individual valuation. The law of diminishing returns records a fact of life, while the norm of marginal utility is a standard of efficient purposive action.

(1) *The Law of Diminishing Returns.* The phenomena of diminishing returns can be illustrated by reference to a stylised picture of farming practice. Suppose that a person sets up a farm with *Land* of X acres, Y of *Capital* (including buildings, implements, livestock, etc.) and a *Labour* force of Z employees. At the end of a working year he notes the total product of the farm, and increases the Labour force to Z + 1 employees. At the end of the second year he finds that the costs in wages of this additional employee are more than balanced by an increase in the total farm produce. He goes on increasing the Labour force; but at a certain stage—say with the employment of Z + 3 workers—the additional return in total produce does not balance the additional cost of employing the + 3rd worker. If he continues adding + 4, then + 5 and + 6, he will find that the additional total product continually diminishes relatively to the costs of the successive additions to the Labour force. The law of diminishing returns is operating. The combination of X Land, Y Capital and Z + 2 Labour gave the optimum return on the total costs. With Land and Capital remaining the same, diminishing returns set in with a Labour force of Z + 3 and continued with every further addition. The farming enterprise was becoming less and less efficient

through over-manning. The same law would, of course, operate if, Land and Labour remaining the same, the Capital factor had been increased beyond the optimum point; or if, Capital and Labour remaining the same, the Land factor had been increased beyond the optimum point.

This, as I have said, is a stylised picture, and the well informed may point out necessary qualifications in detail; but it is hoped that the meaning of 'the law of diminishing returns' has been sufficiently explained. When an end has to be produced by a combination of different means factors, the efficiency of the enterprise depends on the factors being utilised in the right proportions. Hence various possible combinations will be evaluated in relation to the product of the enterprise as a whole.

(2) *The Norm of Marginal Utility*. Obviously a rational being will react to the phenomena of diminishing returns by experimenting with various factoral combinations to get the most profitable one, and this introduces us to the idea of 'marginal utility'. Returning to our farming illustrations, and bearing in mind the highly stylised nature of the argument, we can say that marginal utility refers to the last unit which should be added to Land rather than to Labour or Capital, and the last unit which should be added to Capital rather than to Land or Labour, and the last unit which should be added to Labour rather than to Land or Capital in order to reach the optimum combination.

But marginal utility can best be illustrated if we take, not a case where a combination of different means is required for the production of a given end, but a case in which the end is a complex of parts, each of which is essential for the whole but capable of independent production.

Let us suppose that a multimillionaire decides to found a university capable of providing for 5000 students of the basic faculties. He appoints a competent body to undertake the planning, giving them a ceiling of £X million to finance the scheme. They design lecture rooms, tutorial suites, laboratories, library, assembly hall, hostels, etc. But when the whole complex is costed, it is found that the £X million is inadequate. No more being forthcoming, the plan has to be pared down. It would obviously be foolish to start building library or hostels or laboratories according to the original plans and carrying on until funds had become exhausted. The rational course would be to scale down the project, and consequently each of its constituent parts, to produce a balanced complex even although it was less satisfactory in any particular than in the original scheme.

Let us put the principle here involved in a more abstract form. Suppose that for a given project the total needs or demands can be symbolically represented by 15A, 9B and 6C. If a person has exactly enough means at his disposal (30 units of purchasing power) to meet the demands in full, there is no need for him to evaluate alternative ways of employing his resources. But if—and this is so in the vast majority of cases—the resources fall short of the required amount (he has, let us say, 20 units), then he will have to distribute scarce resources for the satisfaction of competing demands. He may, of course, be an improvident fellow who recklessly squanders his means, but we are supposing him to be a responsible person who acts only after deliberation. If so, he will aim at the maximum realisation of the project as a whole; and maximum realisation means the nearest approach to equilibrium in the fulfilment of the constituent parts of the project. This will require a distribution of resources, not by simple equality, but by proportionate equality over the competing demands. That is to say, with initial demands of 15A, 9B and 6C, a rational being will aim, not at 7A, 7B and 6C, but at 10A, 6B and 4C.

Expressing this in technical terms, we can say that a rational valuation takes place in accordance with the norm of marginal utility. The marginal units are the 10thA, 6thB and 4thC; and they are so called because the person would prefer a 10thA to a 7thB or 5thC, a 6thB to an 11thA or 5thC, and a 4thC to an 11thA or 7thB. This is the allocation which is the most economical because it secures maximum realisation of the project as a whole.

It is not suggested that resources can invariably be allocated in this precise way. Neither demands nor resources are infinitely divisible. Probably all that we can ever get is a rough approximation to an economical solution. But the 'norm' is that to which a rational being aspires and follows to the best of his ability in the given circumstances.

3 INTEGRITY

Remarks on this concept can be fairly brief. While Economy is concerned with the discriminating use of means for a certain complex of ends, it is called into play only because the complex is valued as a whole. That anything—be it a material complex or a productive activity—should be valued in its wholeness implies a third concept which may be called Integrity. This would seem to be the appropriate name since a whole is an integrated totality of parts or members, a perfect whole including all that is essential and excluding everything irrelevant.

While the concept of Economy refers to the production of a balanced whole, that whole may be valued primarily as a means to an end. Thus the building of a university in accordance with the precepts of Economy is the creation of a means to the training of young men and women for the enhancement of the quality of community life. But a whole may be valued for itself and not simply as a means to some further end. Chairs are valued as means; but the possessor of an incomplete set of antique chairs will often devote much time and expense to completing the set just to make it complete. The set is valued as a whole for itself. This is a valuation under the concept of Integrity.

That this concept is not reducible to that of Utility or Economy is evident from the fact that a complex such as a mediaeval abbey can be valued, not only as useful for worship and for the economical allocation of space to meet the varied requirements of the religious order, but also for its architectural grace. Integrity is the concept which governs our attribution of beauty to a work of art, style in speech or writing, the grandeur of military display and the purity of personal character.

Indeed, when we consider the three concepts together—i.e. Utility, Economy and Integrity—it becomes clear that their order of priority is, in one sense, precisely the opposite of that in which we have expounded them. It is the valuation of a complex in its wholeness which calls into play the concept of Economy in the distribution of scarce means for the balanced realisation of the complex end; and Economy governs the extent to which the promptings of Utility will be followed in the use of means for any particular constituent of the complex. That this should be the order of priority is in full accord with the nature of valuation in general as described above (pp. 8–9): it is a volitional attitude directed to the creation and conservation of a pattern of objectives through the pursuit of a further objective which then becomes itself a constituent of the general scheme.

4 'SELF-REALISATION'

Valuations under the concepts of Utility, Economy and Integrity all have one thing in common: they are directed to the production or maintenance of some identifiable objective. A mower is useful for producing a tidy lawn; funds are economically distributed for founding a university complex; the purchase and repair of a chair seen in a junk-shop achieves the integrity of a Chippendale set. This being so, it may well be thought that all valuation is ultimately directed to a supreme objective. Indeed many philosophers have taken this view and sought to identify and define the *Summum Bonum*, the supreme good. According to one school it is pleasure. The theologians have also made their contribution, as when we are told that 'The Chief End of man is to glorify God and to enjoy Him for ever.' But neither of these, nor any other proposed answer, has been generally approved.

However, failure to identify a supreme good has not rendered the individual's life pattern incoherent; and the degree of coherence implies some co-ordinating factor: if not the vision of a supreme objective end, then a subjective factor in the form of an integrating power intrinsic to our own nature.

The problem is well illustrated on the social plane. When the Chancellor of the Exchequer presents his budget, he allocates money for various purposes— general administration, defence, public health, local government aid, pensions, education, the arts, industrial enterprises, and many others. And he explains how he proposes to get the money to finance all these things, levying taxes from various sources. The selection of objectives and proposed levies are interdependent inasmuch as what he proposes to collect as revenue is partly conditioned by the things he wants to support, and the things he thinks he can support are conditioned by the amount of money he thinks he can collect.

Yet, with all this variety of things to be supported and financial sources on which to draw, the Chancellor has so calculated his budget that he can be faced by critical issues if the Commons reject any of its details. Getting it passed virtually unaltered is important because it is considered by him to be a coherent plan for—for what? No doubt he would say 'for the country's good'; and there would be complete agreement that this ought to be his aim. But there might be heated debate as to whether his measures were effectively directed to this end.

The debate, however, would not centre on the question whether an objective, 'the country's good', were being promoted. It would fasten on specific items considered on their merits in relation to other items considered on *their* merits. Had the Chancellor made too little provision for defence, or too much for defence and too little for the health service? Was he strangling productive industry and personal initiative by vicious taxation to support an inefficient bureaucracy? While insisting, if directly challenged in so many words, that his proposals were for the good of the country, his actual defence would be that they constituted a coherent pattern. The pattern would not be defended by reference to an identifiable objective called 'the country's good'. The defence would be the claim that the allocation to the various purposes was fair and reasonable. Its alleged fairness and reasonableness would not look to an objective *Summum Bonum* but would represent his own assessment of relative values.

When it is said that the individual is planning for personal 'happiness', this is a phrase of the same order as the Chancellor's 'good of the country'. The individual's system of values is not governed by the idea of an all-comprehensive objective end. His system is a relatively close or loose federation of subsystems, the unifying factor being his own volitional nature. While each value group must have a firm nucleus as a necessary condition of effective action, it must also have open boundaries, subject to influences from other value groups cherished by the same person.

It may fairly be claimed that we have now established the first part of our thesis concerning the foundations of a moral order. The values pursued by a member of such an order must have their source in his own nature. The idea that goodness in the ultimate sense is an intrinsic property of the thing or action to which it is attributed cannot stand up to examination; and the idea that all values derive from an objective *Summum Bonum* finds no support in practical experience. Valuation is primarily a conative, not a cognitive activity, a volitional attitude expressing approval of some thing as an actual or potential constituent of a system of ends. The initial material for the content of such a system is assimilated from the individual's social environment; and it is progressively supplemented and modified by increasing knowledge and contact with other cultures. Such material, however, cannot be the content of a system of values except as organised by Practical Reason. Characteristic operations of Practical Reason are those which we indicate by the concepts Utility, Economy and Integrity. But Reason is an attribute of the self as a whole, and it operates not only in the organisation of sub-systems but also in the processes whereby they are adjusted one to another. As the centre from which all this activity flows, the member of the moral order is himself the source of his overall pattern of values.

It is interesting that one of the most important—perhaps the greatest—of the 19th century British moral philosophers, namely T H Green, referred to the supreme good as 'self-realisation'. The phraseology is misleading, suggesting that self-realisation is an end at which we aim. But given a subjective interpretation, it is completely appropriate to describe the creative expression of the individual's personality in the pursuit and realisation of ends.

CHAPTER FOUR

The Spiritual Attribute of Personality

We come now to the second precondition of a moral order, namely that its members should be able not only to develop systems of value and adjust them to recognised rules, but also to initiate and direct appropriate changes in the material world. Two questions arise: *first*, What attribute or attributes must pertain to the nature of a being capable of constructing a system of values and conforming to rules? *second*, How can the activities of such a being be described as initiating and directing events in the material world? The first of these questions will be discussed in the present chapter.

1. THE LEGAL AND PSYCHOLOGICAL CONCEPTION OF PERSONALITY
The being to whom we have referred as a member of a moral order is known in law and psychology as a person, personality being ascribed only to those who are self-directing centres of intellect and will and capable of acting in accordance with recognised norms. We shall be concerned here with personality in that very restricted sense alone, concerned only to discover the attribute or attributes which enable a person to evaluate objectives and respect rules.

In *legal theory* it appears that, as originally used by Roman lawyers,[7] personality had substantially the same meaning as in our everyday use. Every human being—man, woman, bond or free—was regarded as a person, it being understood that personality could be more or less complete. Of slaves and those who, from natural infirmity or immaturity, were incapable of participating in legal proceedings, it was said that their personality was incomplete; it was incomplete to the extent that, for one reason or another, they were not fully self-directing. At a later period the stress was increasingly laid on forensic competence, a person signifying one qualified to sue and liable to be sued in the courts. But this was only a change of emphasis, the essential idea throughout being that a person is a self-directing centre capable of recognising and acting in accordance with standards.

The *psychological theory*, though expressed in very different terms is substantially the same. It is true that personality is used in two rather different senses.[8] In a narrow sense it is distinguished from intelligence. We have intelligence tests to ascertain an individual's IQ, while personality tests are concerned with his character, with the system of dispositions that determine his ways of behaving in different situations. In this sense personality seems to be regarded as a sum of particular traits—submission, ascendance; introversion, extroversion; self-seeking, altruism; and so forth. But this suggestion is corrected in the broader sense of the term where stress is on the unity and integrity of normal mental life. Indeed, where such unity is weak or absent we have the pathological condition which, in extreme cases, is known as split personality, two or more mental lives alternating without awareness of each other. Dr Thouless[9] puts the point with admirable clarity. In psychological terms, he says, all volitional activity properly so-called is self- or Ego-directed. In the absence of this central control there could be no responsible behaviour. Mere random conative activity is ineffective in the adaptation to and of environment, and effective adaptation involves observance of rules, the pursuit of general objectives and ideals.

2. THE SPIRITUAL PRE-CONDITION OF KNOWLEDGE

Since 'member of the moral order' may now be equated with 'person' for purposes of our enquiry, we may formulate our question in the following terms: What are the absolutely basic attributes of personality? What are the pre-conditions of intellectual and volitional activity?

We take first the pre-conditions of intellectual activity in the knowledge of a world in time and space.

Awareness of a World in Time. I hear the clock chime 9 and go in to breakfast. The striking of 9 is a succession of events, so that when the first happens the others are non-existent. When the second happens the first no longer exists and the others are still in the future. That is to say, in a temporal succession we have a series of which only one member can exist at any given time. It is present, the others being past or future.

We, however, can be aware of the whole series. There is, therefore, operative in our minds a unifying factor which, as we say, holds together the past, present and future. While the *experienced* members of the series cannot all exist together, they can exist together for the *experiencer*, and they do so without losing their past, present and future distinctiveness (Losing their distinctiveness they would not be a series in time). Clearly, then, the attribute of our minds in virtue of which we can be aware of a temporal succession cannot itself be described in terms of temporal successiveness. This is the inevitable inference because, if our awareness were itself a temporal process, the consciousness of the first event would cease with the event itself, the consciousness of the second vanishing with that event, and so on for the whole series. In this case there could never be the *consciousness of a series*; there would be merely a *series of consciousnesses*. Experience of a series, then, implies the operation of a mental attribute which transcends the limitations of temporal process. In point of fact, our consciousness of time can have no temporal limits. Thus, in the example given, when I hear the first stroke of 9 I shall normally expect the other 8 strokes because I have already heard the clock strike the previous hour.

Awareness of a World in Space. Similarly with regard to my awareness of objects in space. I can never at one and the same time actually perceive all of the room in which I am sitting. I can see most of one wall with its fireplace; then I can turn and look at another wall with its bookshelves, proceed to another with its shelves and desk, and finally look out of the window, I have a series of perceptions of parts of the room, but not of the room. Nonetheless I am able to think them all together as parts of this room. I am aware of living in a three-dimensional world, and in a particular part of it, only in virtue of a synthesising factor in my cognitive activity which unites the discrete perceptions of the parts into an intelligible whole.

3. CONCEPT OF A SPIRITUAL ATTRIBUTE

Since the synthesising factor is a prerequisite of awareness of spacial extension and temporal succession, it cannot itself be described in spacial or temporal terms. That rules out any materialistic designation since the material order is the world in space and time. As distinguished from material, perhaps the least objectionable term will be spiritual since the contrast is familiar in common usage. We may say, then, that a member of a moral order is a being in whom is operative the spiritual attribute of selfhood. Selfhood is the appropriate word because we are talking of a person as a self-directing centre of intellectual activity.

4. THE SPIRITUAL PRE-CONDITION OF VOLITIONAL ACTIVITY

The application of the argument with respect to our conative activity is plain. No one maintains that in rational nature the volitional life proceeds independently of the intellectual. Any act of will, being an overt expression of a value judgement, includes a cognitive reference; and being purposive or teleological it involves awareness of an objective order within which conceived objectives are to be attained. As we have already expressed the point, a rational being does not simply *react* to external events. He *acts* in accordance with the conception of an objective order to which (truly or falsely) he believes those events to belong. This conception of an order in space and time being essential to all volitional activity on the rational level, the spiritual attribute is involved in valuation as in knowledge.

A word of warning may be helpful with regard to the terminology here employed: the term 'spiritual' must not be pressed into the service of metaphysical theories with which it is not concerned. I do not profess to have established the existence of a 'non-material spiritual being' which thinks and wills, a spiritual substance or non-material soul. Such a being may well exist; but any suggestion that its existence is established by my argument is confronted by serious problems. My experience of a clock striking 9 involves the operation of a synthesising, non-temporal attribute, but the experience occupies a measurable tract of time. The striking occupies about 15 seconds on my clock but a considerably longer period on Big Ben. Obviously, experience *in* time and experience *of* time cannot belong to the same universe of discourse. In arguing for an attribute of consciousness (not a conscious being) which cannot be described in spatio-temporal terms we are following the critical method adopted by Kant, requiring the acceptance of a spiritual attribute of selfhood in so far as, but only in so far as it is required to render intelligible our actual experience. It is an epistemological and valuational concept, not the metaphysical one expounded by Kant's successors in Germany and Britain.

CHAPTER FIVE
Causality and Teleology

We have to consider the question: How can the activities of a moral agent be described as initiating and directing material events? That he is active in the material world is not in dispute. What is in question is the idea that his activities initiate and direct physical events in a sense in which none of these events can be said to initiate and direct succeeding events. Thus, if a boy picks up a stone and throws it to break a window, the series of events beginning with the lifting of the stone and ending with the breaking of the window has been initiated by him in order to produce the end result. But if a landslide causes a stone to strike and break a window, no event in this chain of events can be said to have initiated the process in order to produce the broken window. To go beyond this broad formulation of the issue we have to explain the context in which it arises. There is a longstanding dispute as to the sense in which human beings can be held responsible for their actions. It is the controversy of 'Determinism *versus* Free Will (or Libertarianism)'.

Determinism[10] holds that every event which takes place is explicable in causal terms, and that there is no other form of rational explanation. This, it is contended, covers both physical and mental nature. As to the claim that acts of will do not come under causal laws, the answer is that an act of will is an expression of the strongest desire. The strength of this desire derives from the fact that it belongs to a rationalised system of desires. This last sentence agrees, broadly, with what I have said about the nature of valuation and choice in earlier chapters; but the determinist adds that the rationalising activity is a causal process.

Libertarianism[11] seeks to exclude from the universal reign of causality acts of will where a moral issue is at stake. In what is perhaps the most easily expounded form of Libertarianism the doctrine is this: The determinist's account of all valuational activity is correct with one single exception, namely when a person has to choose between performing and transgressing a moral duty. In most day-to-day situations involving a choice between alternatives, serious moral issues do not commonly arise. Whether to buy this hat or that one, a Ford or a British Leyland car, whether to spend one's holiday at home or at a Spanish resort—with regard to questions of this sort one may never feel that it is one's duty to choose in a certain way; and so long as the question of duty does not arise the choice one actually makes (the libertarian concedes) will have been causally determined. But questions of duty do arise. A person may wish to have a holiday in Spain, and he may owe a considerable sum to a builder for work done. His money is insufficient to take the holiday and pay the bill, and so we have a conflict between self-interest and duty. In such a situation, the libertarian says, the person's choice cannot be causally explained. He is responsible for paying the bill—performing the duty. If he chooses to ignore the duty he is blameworthy. That being so, when a moral issue is involved a person must be exercising a free will which operates completely outside the causal process.

The nature of moral choice implied in this libertarian theory will be considered in Chapter Eleven on Moral Responsibility; but it is obvious that the determinist theory is of far wider significance than any controversy which limits the issue to the question of specifically moral choice. If we concede *any* form of voluntary activity to be causally explicable, we are saying that such activity does *not* initiate and direct material events in any sense other than the way in which a stone dislodged from a mountainside can initiate a landslide of scree. And in so far as a person is not an initiator and director of events in the more fundamental sense, to that extent he is not participating in the creation and maintenance of the moral order.

In this chapter, therefore, we are to deal with the nature of voluntary, purposive (teleological) activity in general and the question as to whether it is explicable in causal terms. We begin with an examination of the concept of Causality.

1. CAUSALITY

The 'A Priori' Postulate. The law of causation may be formulated thus: 'For every variation between two events there must be some variation between the antecedent circumstances, without which the variation between the events would not have existed'; or more simply, 'Every event in the space-time order is the effect of some cause'.

How do we know this postulate to be true? The proffered answer is that it can neither be proved nor disproved. It is an *a priori* postulate of all rational thinking.

Hume rejected this contention, arguing on something like the following lines:

We talk as though everything that exists, including the universe itself, must have had a cause. But what do we mean by one thing causing another? We certainly do not perceive any power or force to be operative. What we actually perceive in a so-called causal series is a number of events in temporal succession. When the series is frequently repeated and we become accustomed to the succession, we entertain the idea that each event in the series is the cause of the next in line astern.

(1) Kant on Causality[12]

On examining arguments of this type, Kant agreed that we never do perceive a necessary connexion between any two particular events, but he saw that this is not the point at issue. What the postulate of causal necessity means is that every event in space and time is the effect of *some* cause. Only empirical investigation will reveal what the significant antecedent event or cause was in any given case; but that there is such an event is an *a priori* postulate. It is not a generalisation from experience. It is a basic condition of all experience of an objective order in space and time. That this is so is proved by Hume's own argument, for his explanation of our belief in necessary causal connexion presupposes the very idea to be explained.

According to Hume, experience is a stream of impressions ('passing through the mind' in common parlance). Suppose, then, that I have a stream of 9 impressions. All have an identical form in the sense that they are all my impressions. They can, however, have different contents, according to Hume, in the sense that they can be recognisably different from each other, the differences becoming familiar as the series is repeated time after time. Let us say that my 9 impressions consist of a series of 3 twice repeated:

$$a1, b1, c1; \quad a2, b2, c2; \quad a3, b3, c3.$$

But how is it possible for me to be aware of this as a series of 3 twice repeated and not a single series of 9:

$$a, b, c, d, e, f, g, h, i?$$

I am able to say that it is a series of 3 twice repeated only by distinguishing between (i) the perception of a succession of different entities and (ii) successive perceptions of the same entity, thus:

(ii)
Successive perceptions
of the same thing

(i)
Perception of succession
of different things

$$
\begin{array}{ccc}
\downarrow & \downarrow & \downarrow \\
\rightarrow a1 & b1 & c1 \\
\rightarrow a2 & b2 & c2 \\
\rightarrow a3 & b3 & c3
\end{array}
$$

To draw this distinction between seeing 3 different things in succession and seeing the same thing thrice, I must be attributing my impressions a1,a2,a3 to three grounds or causes, namely three appearances of A which I postulate as an identical something persisting throughout its successive appearances; likewise attributing b1,b2,b3 to the appearances of B, and c1,c2,c3 to the appearances of C.

Hence when Hume talks of the experience of a repeated series of impressions as generating the idea of causal connexion, he fails to note that he could not have had this experience unless he had already postulated causal connexion, assigning appearances of A as causes of the 'a' impressions, and so on. He is, in fact, assuming the validity of the *a priori* postulate.

What Kant has here demonstrated is that one cannot talk intelligibly without assuming an objective order in space and time, and that any attempt to say what happens within that order involves the postulate of 'ground and consequent', the postulate which, in the space-time world, is called 'causality'.

(2) The Nature of Causal Explanation

But to establish the postulate of causality as essential to our awareness of an objective order in space and time is a questionable gain if we then go on to misinterpret its significance. 'Cause' has a wide range of meanings—ground, reason for, manipulative agency, creator, etc. Within philosophy it has had distinct technical meanings. Thus Aristotle distinguished 'efficient cause' (initiating agent), 'formal cause' (what we should call the essential nature), 'material cause' (the matter or content) and 'final cause' (the purpose of the thing's existence). Of these four 'causes', 'efficient cause' is about the nearest to present scientific usage; and in all that follows we shall use the term in its scientific sense.

Cause and Effect as Events. Cause and effect are correlative terms, neither having any meaning apart from the other. The concept of an effect is an event preceded by a cause, a cause being an event preceding an effect. They are correlative *events*, not *things*. As older philosophers would have said, they are not substances but modes, states or activities of substances. When I hear the ringing note of hammer on anvil, the cause is the *striking* of the hammer and the effect is my *hearing*.

Causality not a Force. Causal laws or laws of nature are not powers governing events. They are formulae which we use to describe the ways in which things react, in virtue of their own nature, to the presence and activities of other things constituting their environment. If one billiard ball is driven against another, the effect is the way in which the latter, in virtue of its weight, shape and relation to the condition of the table, will react to the impact.

Causal Inference Retrospective. The formula of the postulate of causality given on p. 30 shews that in causal inference we infer, not *predictively* but *retrospectively*. To understand my hearing a noise, I look around and find its cause in the hammer *having struck* the anvil.

Things react selectively to environment. In any given case when a thing reacts to some circumstance or activity, the significant reaction is not to the total environment but to some particular ingredient or ingredients. If I am struck by a piece of wood, it is the weight rather than the colour which will be causally significant; but it is the colour which will be causally significant if the wood is a direction post.

Causality and Prediction. It is sometimes said that, if we admit the universal applicability of the causal principle, this implies that if one had a complete knowledge of the state of the world at any given point in time, one could, theoretically speaking, predict the whole future course of universal history. No one pretends that this is a practical possibility. It is the theoretical possibility that is supposed to be implied. This is a complete misunderstanding. Causality is a postulate of our attempts to understand what *has* happened. Its eyes are directed exclusively to the past; to the future it is eternally blind. In causal explanation we infer from effect to cause, not from cause to effect. Moreover, its formula 'If the event X happens there must be *some* preceding event or events to which it is the reaction' is not itself any guide as to what the preceding event was, since the reaction of anything which constitutes the 'effect factor' in the cause-effect relationship is not a reaction to the total preceding state of the universe but to some select factor or factors. It is a reaction *in* a total environment *to* a specific factor in that environment. We have to find out by trial and error what the 'cause factor' actually was.

The Uniformity of Nature. The rationality of procedure by trial and error depends on an additional *a priori* postulate, namely that of the uniformity of nature, one which is quite different from that of causality. It would not be incompatible with the causal postulate to say 'Every event has a cause, but precisely the same kind of event could have entirely different types of cause on different occasions'. But if we believed this to be so we should never embark on the search for regular connexions. It is the postulate of uniformity, not that of causality, which induces this search. Apparent multiplicity of causes impels us to distinguish within complex events the factor which is common to them all. When we have discovered this common factor, then on the basis of the postulate of uniformity we can proceed to future prediction.

Limits of Prediction. But even in association with the postulate of uniformity, the limits of possible prediction are substantial. Since experimental trials (with gradual elimination of error) are essential for the discovery of causal sequences, it follows that no *original* prediction (i.e. one which is not merely the prediction of the *repetition* of a sequence already observed) is possible except with regard to the behaviour of something which has been designed to behave in precisely that way. And this designing of the apparatus is itself the fruit of long experiment and discovery of causal sequences. To many of us incredibly, it was successfully predicted that at a certain time on a certain day a man would make the first landing on the moon. But all the stages which lead to such successful predictions are carefully planned to achieve just those results.

(3) The Limits of Causal Explanation

It is not merely as an instrument of prediction that causality, even when taken in conjunction with the postulate of uniformity of nature, is of limited service. There are also limits to its use in explaining what has already happened. That this is so will be admitted when we consider the following points: (i) the postulate of causality is merely one aspect of a more fundamental one, namely the postulate of universal rationality, (ii) causal explanation is concerned only with external relations, and (iii) it conceives of these only in terms of temporal succession.

(i) The General Postulate of Rationality

Every event, we say, is the effect of some antecedent space-time event. But we do not think of the universe as a mere collection of events. This will be plain if we look again at Kant's epistemological refutation of Hume. Anyone claiming to have experienced a series of impressions which have occurred on several occasions (say, a1,a2,a3) is assuming them to be the manifestations of *A*. He thus assumes an objective order to which *A* belongs, and also an experiencer who continues as a self-identical being throughout the temporal succession. And because, as a matter of common experience, the 'a' series is part of a whole order of events in which we can discern causal uniformities, we assume rationality in the objective order to which *A* belongs.

(ii) Causality concerned with External Relations

But while causality presuppoes rational order throughout the material universe, it is concerned only with the external relations of the members of that orderly world. It is never concerned with their inner activities. Thus, I hear the chiming of a clock, the cause being the chiming, the effect being my hearing. But what is the relation of my hearing to *me* as distinguished from its relation to the chiming (of the clock)? What is the nature of the internal activity which is outwardly expressed in the response constituting the effect?

It may be said, 'But we do offer some causal explanation of the internal activity. The impact of the sound waves causes vibrations in my ear-drums, and these vibrations result in impulses being transmitted through the appropriate nerves to the brain'. This explanation, however, proceeds by dividing the 'me' into a number of constituent parts—ear-drums, nervous system, etc.,—the behaviour of the one being an event correlated with an event in the other. This is genuine explanation, enlightening us with respect to the questions we want to have answered. But the method shews that all causal explanation is of an externally correlating kind. However far we go in the process of causally explaining a complex reaction, it is always by the method of dissecting the complex and correlating the events in the separated parts. However far we go in explaining 'internal causality', we never get beyond the formula, 'X, in accordance with its own intrinsic nature, reacts in the form 'a' to the activity 'b' of Y'. Whether it is ever necessary or possible to explain how the intrinsic nature of anything manifests itself in just these ways may be an open question; but if it ever is possible, the explanation cannot be in causal terms.

(iii) Causal Explanation in Terms of Temporal Succession

If we consider any cause-effect relation in actual experience, we find that cause and effect are simultaneous events or two aspects of a single event. Thus, looking out of my window, I see a passing car. The car passing and my seeing it pass belong to one and the same time-span. It may be said that there is a temporal succession inasmuch as there is an infinitesimal interval between the passing of the car and the impinging of the reflected light on the retinas of my eyes. But if we are going in for these refinements, the correct statement will be that the cause-effect correlation is the reaction of my retina to the impinging of the light rays. Again, when a man is cycling along the road, the turning of the pedal-crank, movement of chain and turning of rear wheel are a continuous movement.

But although cause and effect are simultaneous aspects of the one occasion, the world in which they occur would be unintelligible if we did not discern any rational priority of the one over the other. That priority we do discern. We do not think it a matter of indifference whether it is said that the impact of the light induces change in the retina or that the change in the retina induces the impact of light rays. It is not a matter of indifference whether we say that the turning of the pedal-crank induces turning of the rear wheel of the bicycle or *vice-versa*. (In fact, before the invention of the free-wheel gear, the first statement would be correct for ascending, and the second for descending a hill.) Relations of this sort belong to an order of reality which we understand only when, through experience, we are able to view events in a rational order of 'ground and consequent'.

To express this *rational* relationship when dealing with physical events, we express it in *temporal* terms, in terms of causes and effects represented under the concept of a succession in time. That this is exclusively the method of causal explanation is clear from the ways in which philosophers define the concept of causality: 'For every variation between events there must be some variation in the *antecedent* circumstances' (Ross); and 'The cause of a phenomenon is the *antecedent, or concurrence of antecedents*, on which it is invariably and unconditionally *consequent*' (Mill). (The italics in all cases are mine) As to the propriety of this mode of explanation, there can be no question. It expounds rational priorities in a way eminently suitable for the material world. But the nature of the method must be borne in mind when we are considering the limitations of causal explanation. It is an analogical method, rational priorities being expressed in terms of temporal succession. If there is anything in our experience which cannot be rationally explained in terms of temporal succession, then it cannot be explained on the causal principle.

2. TELEOLOGY
There is, in fact, a wide range of experience which cannot be explained in causal terms and for which purposive or teleological concepts are required.
(1) Teleological Explanation as Projective
Let us suppose that a man acquires a car, never having owned one before. He will probably take a short course of instruction on the machine, particularly on the working of an internal-combustion engine. The whole course will consist of explanations in causal terms. What makes the wheels go round? Transmission of energy through the driving-shaft. Why is it that, precisely when it is needed, there is a spark from the plug in the cylinder-head? The distributor of the electrical charges is controlled by a shaft which links with the movement of the piston; and so forth. Any question about what is happening is answered by reference to another happening in some part of the machine. It is true that the machine has been designed by man to perform as it does, but this has nothing to do with explaining why any *specific* event in the working of the car engine happens when and as it does.

But the new owner will also take a course of instruction on how to drive the car. Let us say that the instructions to get the car moving on the road go something like this:

waggle your gear-lever to ensure that it is in neutral; check that the hand-brake is on; pull out choke; switch on ignition; operate starter; return choke; push out clutch; engage first gear; release hand-brake; ease in clutch and increase acceleration.

This is an intelligible sequence of actions which will normally result in the desired end, namely the movement of the car along the road. It is an intelligible but not a causal series. Each one of the actions directed by the instructor is part of *a* causal series, but the ten actions are not themselves a causal series.

Looking for such causal series as do occur, let us start with the end product, the actual movement of the car. In the total situation the specific cause was the closing of the clutch. The cause of this was the release of pressure on the clutch-pedal. The cause of this release was a muscular movement; and the further regressive causal events can be explained, if at all, only by the physiologist. So we leave that causal series and go back to the preceding one, the releasing of the hand-brake. The cause was a muscular movement leading us once more into the realm of physiology. The same is true of every one of the ten prescribed actions. Each is part of *a* causal series leading straight into our physiological makeup; and if the ten actions are in fact causally related, it can only be because they all belong to a vast complex occurring in the body of the agent. And it will be a causal complex completely beyond his own knowledge, none of the actions having been performed because it was known to be part of the complex.

On the other hand, the agent is completely aware of the immediate *effects* which will result from his actions. Releasing the clutch-pedal will close the clutch; releasing the handbrake will clear the road-wheels, and so on. That is to say, he is aware of each action as the initiation of a causal process, and he performs it for that reason. He is also aware why the ten actions are taken in the prescribed order. This is the order which will set the car moving on the road. In short, the ten actions of the series have no intelligible (or at least no known) connexions *retrospectively* as a causal series, but they have intelligible connexions *projectively* as a pattern of means to an end.

(2) Teleological Explanation as Internal

Causal explanation, as we have already seen, is from an external point of view. It is concerned with the action and reaction of A in relation to B. The antithetic character of causal and teleological explanation is emphasised by the fact that valuation and choice in any form are excluded from any experiment investigating causes. The experiment is, of course, set up by a rational being for a purpose; but what he does is to observe how things actually behave under certain pre-arranged conditions. He can, when investigating the cause of malaria, infect an organism with the mosquito toxic culture, but whether this produces malaria is a matter of fact and not of anyone's choice. The paradigm of a causal relationship is not a teleological activity but an inorganic or low grade organic process.

While causal explanation is thus from an external point of view, the very opposite holds with regard to teleological explanation, for purposiveness can be known only from inner experience. It is an activity which envisages an end product as the culmination of a series of measures occupying a tract of time. It therefore involves the synthesising process of valuation under one or more of the concepts of Practical Reason. That an activity of this kind cannot be explained from the point of view of the external observer is so obvious that the argument need not be laboured.

(3) Teleology a Non-Temporal Activity

It must be equally obvious that purposive activity cannot be explained on any analysis for which the concept of temporal succession is basic. Purposive activity covers a series of actions directed to the securing of an end. You can explain why you are performing those actions by reference to the proposed end; but your explanation as to why you are engaging in the activity is not an explanation of the nature of the activity itself. Purposive activity depends on the power of holding together in a unitary consciousness the end *and* the series of actions leading to its realisation. This power of holding together can be described only in terms of the non-temporal attribute of selfhood explained in Chapter Four, an attribute which has no place in the vocabulary of causality.

If, after all this discussion, anyone still entertains the idea that the voluntary activities of a rational being are ultimately explicable in causal terms, the following point must surely rid him of the illusion. There is at least one rational activity which cannot be causally explained, namely causal explanation itself. The ability to explain events causally, i.e. in terms of temporal succession, implies the ability to be aware of temporal succession. But, as we have seen in considering the nature of personality, the awareness of a series of events in time involves, as essential to that awareness, a synthesising activity which is not itself reducible to a temporal series.

(4) Teleology and Causal Process

While causality and teleology are completely different concepts, the difference does not make for conflict. The one refers to the relations between events in the material world of space and time, while the other refers to the ways in which a rational being manipulates a complex of events in accordance with his system of values. They do not stand in opposition to each other because, while there can be causal process without purposive activity, wherever there is teleological activity there is causal process. In so far as it is operative in the material world, teleological activity consists in the manipulation of material things, in the initiation, co-ordination and termination of causal processes.

Obviously there remains the problem of explaining how the purpose of a rational being which does not itself belong to the causal order is able to initiate and direct a causal process. This is an issue which lies outside the domain of moral philosophy. The task of the moral theorist is to expound the main structure of the moral order and to lay bare its essential foundations. Of these foundations, one is the ability of a moral agent to initiate and direct causal processes by a power which is not itself explicable in causal terms. That the moral agent does in fact initiate and control events over a large area of the material world is a matter of everyday experience, and we have shewn that the power exercising this control is explicable in teleological, not in causal, terms. It is not part of our task to go beyond this and explain *how* a power teleological in character can exercise this control. That task pertains to a quite different line of enquiry.

At the same time, moral philosophy cannot be isolated from other philosophical and psycho-physical studies which have a bearing on the nature of its essential foundations; and so it may be worth suggesting the area in which the teleological-causal problem may be most fruitfully explored. It is the area in which the relationship is mediated through organic life. While teleological control is most evident in such enterprises as putting a car on the road, building an aeroplane or an orchestral performance, in every case the initial stages of the activity are traced back to causal processes within the human body. This has long been recognised in the history of philosophy, the issue being posed in accordance with the assumptions made. Thus, on the assumption that we are concerned with two substantive entities, mind and matter, some philosophers have tried to find a particular point of contact between mind and brain while others have adopted the theory of psycho-physical parallelism, holding that the two streams of phenomena, material events and mental states, proceed independently. Rejecting the 'two substances' assumption, one school would reduce all mental phenomena to forms of physical activity (Materialism), while another would consider all material existence as 'a concatenation of ideas' (Idealism).

None of these traditional theories has proved satisfactory, and it will be necessary to find a fresh approach. Instead of posing our problem in terms of substances, mind and matter, which are to be related to each other, or reduced one to the other, it will be better to start with the fact that two kinds of activity—material (causal) and spiritual (teleological)—take place in the one body, a highly developed organism to the activities of which causal concepts are only partially relevant. At certain levels it is impossible to explain organic behaviour except in quasi-teleological terms. It may therefore be that the relationship of causal process to teleological activity can best be explained by an elucidation of the nature of organic life.

However that may be, we have now completed our own survey of the foundations of a moral order. There are two basic conditions of its existence. First, the values cherished by its members must have their source in the nature of the members themselves, as explained in chapters One to Three. Second, in the pursuit of these values as disciplined by social norms, the activities of the members must be the initiators and directors of events in the material world, not mere events in the causal process. That condition has been covered in chapters Four and Five; and having surveyed the foundations, we proceed to explore the structure of the moral order itself.

PART TWO

Positive Law and the Moral Ideal

CHAPTER SIX

Practical Moral Attitudes

As explained in the Introduction, we shall concentrate on the nature of positive law and the moral ideal because positive law is especially illuminating with respect to the concepts employed in a normative order, and the moral ideal is our ultimate standard of right and wrong. Let us look first, however, at whatever guidance may be offered by practical moral attitudes since it is these attitudes we wish to interpret in the sense of elucidating their governing principles.

1. MORAL JUDGEMENT AS ULTIMATE JUDGEMENT ON VOLUNTARY ACTION

Valuation in general is the creative expression of personality. We do not, however, value things in general. We evaluate them on specific grounds in given contexts, and here we are concerned with the assessment known as moral judgement.

The word 'moral' is used in different senses, and so we must first explain the sense in which it is to be employed throughout the following pages. In its basic significance as ordinarily used, 'moral judgement' means 'the ultimate judgement' on the action or proposed action of a voluntary agent. This interpretation does not prejudge the question as to the supreme standard of right and wrong or the source of this standard. Whatever may be the truth on these matters, we are at present only accepting the assumption that 'moral' is to be equated with 'ultimate'. When, in a given situation, all the *pros* and *cons* have been weighed and you say, 'This is what ought to be done', or 'That must not be done', you are affirming a moral judgement. The assessment may have been very difficult to make, and one may be very conscious of the fact that it could be mistaken. Is membership of the armed forces compatible with allegiance to the Christian faith? This is a much debated issue; and a person who decides it in one way may have done so with great hesitation and subsequently come to believe that his decision was mistaken. But when he has decided that, on balance, the argument favours this rather than that side, this decision is *prima facie* his ultimate judgement on the issue as seen there and then, the one he is morally bound to implement in practice.

It should be noted that I call this a merely *prima facie* moral judgement. I do so because men often make pronouncements which implicitly claim but do not in fact have this finality. In almost any area of public or social life we find some individual saying 'I take this decision on principle' without explaining what the principle is. He may mean 'because this is party policy' or 'this is what my union has decided' or 'this is what my church demands'. He is deciding on the basis of a particular sectional allegiance. But the moral order is potentially coextensive with humanity or rational nature universally. Consequently any principle which can govern a moral judgement must be one which can have the allegiance of rational nature universally. The politician's or trade unionist's or Christian's decision can be a genuine ultimate judgement only if the principle appealed to reflects a standard which can have the allegiance of mankind universally.

What, then, can claim to be the ultimate standard in questions of right and wrong?

2. SOME SUGGESTED CRITERIA

When we pass beyond general agreement on the status of moral judgement and ask about the standard or standards by which moral right and wrong are assessed, we get a variety of apparently different answers; Intuition, Conscience, Equity, the Will of God. But when the answers are genuine attempts to answer the question the differences are more apparent than real.

Intuition. There is a theory called Intuitionism which holds that rightness and wrongness are qualities which, on careful inspection, we just 'see' to be in the action itself. It is thus on all fours with the theory of 'intrinsic goodness' considered and rejected in Chapter One. It is mentioned here only because there is a practical attitude which seems to give it some countenance. A person may say 'I just *see* this action to be right (wrong), and I neither can nor need give reasons for saying so.' If this is not merely an impatient evasion, if the conviction is maintained over a period and in varying circumstances, we can be virtually certain that it has some foundation which could be laid bare by a judicious use of the Socratic technique. But if the person really can give no reason for pronouncing an action to be morally right (or wrong), then there is no norm to which the pronouncement is relevant and, despite the language in which it is couched, it has no relevance to the moral order. Bare alleged intuition must therefore be left out of account when we are looking for suggested criteria.

Conscience. The appeal to conscience implies belief in an internal tribunal overriding any external authority; and a person adopting this attitude will usually be prepared to offer reasons for his conviction, as for instance when a conscientious objector during the late war would defend his position before a national service tribunal. The defence might be on straightforward humanist lines—all wars are wrong as increasing the threat to general happiness rather than protecting it, the plea here being founded on some such vague idea as the wellbeing of mankind generally. There are here two implicit assumptions which, on being made explicit, postulate a range of values cherished by mankind and some imperative demanding their promotion. For the humanist the imperative comes from man's own nature while for the theist it is the will of God.

Equity. The humanist interpretation of the moral imperative is, in essence, an appeal to equity, and since the alternative concepts are equity and the will of God, the question is whether there is any significant relationship between the two.

The will of God. This is the proffered criterion with by far the richest content; but the appeal to the divine will has different meanings. There is the familiar *dictum* 'The moral life consists in obedience to the will of God for the sake of eternal happiness'. This is not really an acceptance of God's will as the supreme standard, the ultimate appeal being to self-interest. The meaning is concealed by the assumption that God has absolute power over creation, obedience being the only sure road to eternal happiness. The assumption, apparently, is not universally accepted. There was an old Irish lady who judiciously hedged her bets by always bowing, not only at the name of Jesus but also at that of Satan. On being reprimanded she explained 'It costs you nothing to be polite to the Old Gentleman, and you can never be sure where you'll be after landing at the end of things'.

The far more significant form of the appeal to divine will is on a very different level. The familiar language of religious worship expresses an absolute surrender to the divine will, but this is characteristic only of monotheistic religions such as modern Judaism, Christianity and Islam. It is by no means true of religion universally; and to put the issue in perspective we have to look lt different levels of the religious consciousness. As moral concepts become increasingly associated with the divine nature there is a corresponding increase in devotional allegiance.

Animism and Polytheism. In Animism and primitive Polytheism the gods and spirits are, for the most part, shadowy and vaguely personalised forces, some friendly, others the reverse; and when they are credited with significant powers, propitiation rather than devotion plays a considerable part in the ritual. In that stage ethical considerations can play but a small part in the relations between gods and men; and a little sharp practice on either side is not out of place if it can be effected with impunity. These remarks do not, of course, present the whole picture as is evident from the literature of classical Greece. But even in the sophisticated Polytheism of the Greeks, the gods exhibit the virtues and vices of mortals. The Olympians often engaged in domestic scandal and other irregularities calculated, according to Plato, to corrupt the life of any decent city. So far from providing good examples they stood sadly in need of them.

Henotheism is the name applied to the level of religion which, while accepting the existence of many gods, affirms a special relationship with one. The patriarchs and Israelites of the Exodus were henotheists in this sense. Yahweh had the exclusive right to their allegiance and they were his chosen people.

There is a strong temptation to read back into this period the outlook of later Jewish monotheism, and to represent the attitude of the colonists of Canaan as one of unconditional allegiance to their god. It was far from being so. The obedience was not unconditional but governed by covenant, the relation being analogous to that of feudal lord and vassal. Yahweh was sovereign lord to

whom the Israelites were bound to render homage and service in return for the
land of Canaan. The term 'covenant' was understood in its ordinary sense,
binding both parties to observe ethical standards; but it was accepted that
either party might be tempted to default. The people might be charged and
punished for disobedience, and Yahweh might become lax in the defence of
his people. The moral norms were standards which lord and people ought to
obey but which they were both capable of ignoring. On one occasion, we are
told, Yahweh confirmed his promise to Abraham, binding himself by the use
of an old Semitic ritual.[1] This, apparently, gave Abraham more confidence that
the promise would be kept.

Monotheism supersedes henotheism when ultimate moral principles are
conceived, not as norms to which the divine will *ought* to conform but as
expressing *intrinsic attributes* of the divine nature itself, attributes which
necessarily govern the expression of its will. It is at this stage, and at this stage
alone, that the religious attitude is expressed in terms of absolute, unqualified
obedience. But this is clearly an allegiance which bows neither to overwhelming
power nor to omniscience, but rather to the moral perfection with which they
are associated.

What, then, are the moral attributes intrinsic to the divine nature? Various
ones are mentioned, but pre-eminent is the attribute of Justice with which
Equity is apparently synonymous.

Justice and judgement are the habitation of thy throne (*Ps.* 89 v. 14)

The Lord cometh to judge the earth. With righteousness
shall he judge the world, and the people with equity (*Ps.* 98 v. 9)

Thus saith the Lord, Keep ye judgement and do justice (*Isai.* 56 v. 1)

Thus saith the house of Israel, The way of the Lord is not
equal. O, house of Israel, are not my ways equal? Are not
your ways unequal? (*Ezekiel,* 18 v. 29)

And we have the definition,

God is a Spirit, infinite, eternal and unchangeable in his
being, wisdom, power, holiness, justice, goodness and truth.
(*Shorter Catechism* of the Westminster Assembly)

Omitting the claim to immediate intuition of the rightness of acts, a claim
which indicates no norm, there is a fairly solid consensus as to the nature of the
moral standard. For the mature religious consciousness it appears to be justice
or equity, and the appeal to conscience, if not an indirect appeal to the will of
God, appears to be an appeal to equity.

The principal aim of the present chapter has been to see whether we can
identify a generally accepted standard of moral right and wrong. Granted that
only an approximate answer can be elicited from the foregoing rapid survey of
what people seem to accept as the standard, it does indicate something of a
consensus centred on the idea of justice. Intuition being irrelevant as admitting
no standard at all, we are left with Conscience, Equity and The Will of God.

Conscience appears to have significance only as implyng either the criterion of equity or subordination to the will of God, and the specifically moral attribute of the divine will is taken to be equity or justice.

This gives us a firmly established point of departure from which we can survey the relations between the positive law of the State and the moral ideal, the idea of justice being central to both. In the next chapter we shall be looking at the main concepts of positive law, with particular attention to the way in which they constitute the framework of a normative system within the moral order.

CHAPTER SEVEN

Justice and Positive Law

'Justice' is administered in the State courts through the interpretation and application of rules of law when the State courts are adjudicating on claims of right. We are referring here to civil law as distinguished from criminal law since it is in the civil context that the structure of a legal system is best seen.

There are many different legal orders: the positive law of the State, the ecclesiastical law of a church, the professional codes of doctors and lawyers, and moral law. But certain concepts are common to all, and in the positive law of the State we have a legal order in which these concepts have been systematically employed and defined as in no other system.

1. LAW, RIGHT AND DUTY

Many languages, and apparently all the main European ones, have two names for a system of legal rules. In Latin we have *Jus* and *Lex,* in French *Droit* and *Loi*, in German *Recht* and *Gesetz*, and down to the early seventeenth century at least, we had in English *Right* and *Law.* The terms are sometimes used interchangeably; but when they are distinguished, Lex, Loi, Gesetz and Law tend to stress the legislative element, the content derived, for example, from the statutes of a mediaeval king or enactments of a modern parliament; while Jus, Droit, Recht (and earlier English Right) tend to refer to the whole body of the legal system as derived from various sources, especially ancient custom and judicial decision as well as from legislation. This wider sense of the legal order is the more fundamental. *Lex* is but a late product of literacy; *Jus* is as old as mankind. Long before legislation in our sense was practised, communities had quite elaborate systems of law consisting of immemorial custom interpreted and developed by judicial decisions and the teaching of hereditary jurisconsults such as the 'brehons' of Ireland.

Rather unexpectedly, law in this fundamental sense does not, in its very early stages, have our modern explicit contrast between right and duty.[2] The reason will be understood if we look at the ancient form of society[3] as found, for example, in Anglo-Saxon England or Celtic Ireland, Scotland and Wales. Social institutions were then still based predominantly on bonds of kinship rather than on the fact of common residence within a given territory. Naturally, common residence played an important part inasmuch as the societies in question were not nomadic tribes but settled communities engaged in agriculture, animal husbandry and commerce; but for long ages after the beginnings of permanent territorial occupation their institutions were dominated by the older conception of society as a kindred. In these circumstances the legal order differed from ours in two important respects.

First, ancient law was wide ranging in ways different from our own, covering the activities of kings, nobles, commoners, churchmen, physicians, bards, etc; and especially relevant to ethical theory is the fact that there was no general acceptance of a distinction between legal judgements of the communal courts and moral judgements of the individual conscience.

Secondly—and this is what prevented any clear recognition of the distinction between right and duty—the individual was not, technically speaking, a person in the eyes of the law. He did not *qua* individual have any rights or duties, for *qua* individual he was not even a member of the community. Membership derived from membership of a family group. In ancient Ireland the comprehensive family group was the *Fine*,[4] consisting of those descended in the male line from a common great-great-grandfather, the members being jointly responsible in varying degrees for redressing the wrongs done by any of their number. As each male, on coming of age, would acquire a portion of land and perform the appropriate military service, we moderns would distinguish among the consequences of his majority the right to a tenement of land and the duty of military service. But neither he nor his contemporaries thought in that way. Becoming a householder and performing military service, with all the other details incidental to his position, were simply the man's undivided status acquired on reaching majority. There is, in fact, a Gaelic word *dlighe*, a blanket term covering law or right or duty as the context requires, a term which seems to reflect just this early notion of status.

2. RIGHTS IN GENERAL

As the importance of the family group gradually diminished relatively to the requirements of common residence, the individual *qua* individual acquired increased standing until, at length, he became recognised as a 'person' in himself. Concurrently there emerged an explicit distinction between rights and duties.

It is a remarkable fact that, when this stage of legal development is reached, the name for law in general, is also used to signify the individual's rights—not his duties but his rights, not what is demanded of him but what he may legitimately demand. This is apparently no linguistic accident, as is evident from the extent to which the priority of 'right' dominates legal thinking. *Jus, droit* and *recht* all acquired the double meaning, while in English *right* in the secondary sense has virtually displaced the primary one. That a principle is here operative is clear from the fact that our courts of justice regard their function as the vindication of rights, directly in ordinary civil actions and indirectly in criminal cases. This attitude is reflected in the books. Thus a person may be referred to in an abbreviated form as 'a subject of rights', the law of persons may be expounded under the heading 'rights and attributes', and Stair, defining the content of a legal system, says that 'the formal and proper objects of law are the rights of men'.[5]

Definition of right. What, then, is a right? It may be defined as 'A legally recognised sphere of autonomy for one person which entails a demand with respect to the behaviour of some other person or persons'. 'Autonomy' here means that the one possessing the right has complete legal freedom to act or refrain from acting as he pleases—within the allotted sphere. Thus, if he has the right to take sand and gravel from a certain river estuary, he is not bound to take the material (to be bound would be to have a duty); he is free to take or leave. But if he wishes to take, others are under a duty not to obstruct him, and some may be under an obligation to render postive assistance. From the existence of his right their duty necessarily follows.

This is a comprehensive definition of 'right'; but rights fall into different categories of which three are significant for our purposes.[6] They are 'personal right', 'real right' and 'basic right'; and from reflection on the last we are led to consideration of the preconditions of all rights.

(a) *Personal right* in the technical sense (*jus ad rem,* right *to . . .*) arises from some special relationship between the holder of the right and the ower of the duty. Thus, if I make an agreement with a coal merchant for the delivery of a quantity of fuel at a certain price, I have a right against him personally to the delivery of the fuel, and he has a right to payment against me personally. Examples could be reeled off indefinitely since rights of this kind constitute a social jigsaw of reciprocal rights and duties integrating the individual with his fellows. What is common to them all is their origin in a special relationship which is often, though not necessarily always, created by the persons concerned. My right to delivery of the fuel is against this particular merchant, Mr A B, and not against anyone else. His duty is to deliver it to me and (so far as the duty is based on the agreement) to no one else. A duty correlative to a personal right may be termed an obligation, but we need not adopt this refinement.

(b) *Real Right* in the technical sense (*jus in re*, right *in . . .*) is best understood in the form of ordinary property right. Once the load of fuel has been delivered to my house, it is my property, and no one—no one—is entitled to use or remove it without my permission. The right to its delivery was exclusively against the coal merchant. The right to its remaining with me is a right not only against him but against the world. Again, if I own an area of land, then (subject to the relevant rules of law) I have a right 'against the world' prohibiting occupation or use without my permission. It is true that the duties correlative to real rights are negative rather than positive. All the world is not required to do something to or for the person owning the right. The requirement is to refrain from doing something, namely interfering with the subject-matter of the right.

Both real rights and personal rights exist only within a community of interdependent members. A person's real rights are not only protected but are also delimited by law, the delimitation being modified from time to time in accordance with changing circumstances, economic necessity and political ideology. He therefore belongs to a community of interdependent members in the sense that there must be a general will directed to the maintenance of the normative order as it exists at any given time.

But real rights are more fundamental than personal ones inasmuch as the latter are more specifically conditioned. The real rights pertaining to a man within the social order are defined or catalogued with respect to their subject-matter and not with respect to his relations with other persons. Personal rights, on the other hand, are defined in terms of the acts or forbearances of others in relation to him. The interdependence is not merely as between him and the general will; it is also specifically as between him and some other person or persons.

Real rights are also more fundamental in that personal rights can exist only as secondary to real rights. The coal merchant must have a real right to the fuel and I must have a real right to the money before we can agree to the exchange.

It will therefore be evident that both real and personal rights are dependent on the possession of power. The owner of land must have acquired the relevant rights through inheritance or purchasing power; and the possessor of a personal right must have had some particular influence sufficient to induce the other party to undertake the obligation.

(c) *Basic Rights*. But we also recognise what are called basic rights which arise, not from the possession of power but from human need. This implies a quasi-juridical order transcending the limits of institutionalised society. That its existence is not a discovery by modern man is shewn by the laws of ancient peoples regarding treatment of 'the stranger within the gates'. What was regarded as due to the stranger was, admittedly, not an extensive range of rights, but the basis of the recognition, human need, was the same as that with which we now associate the idea of basic rights—the right of the immature to nurture and protection, the right to earn a living by the use of one's talents, to maintenance during unemployment or for old age, and so forth.

What is noteworthy about such proclaimed basic rights is that, while they can be implemented only in an institutionalised society, and incorporated for the most part in positive law, their 'rightfulness' is deemed to come initially, not from the positive law itself but from a quasi-juridical order which challenges the positive law to incorporate them.

It is true that the notion of basic rights cannot be distinctly formulated by men in primitive societies. It emerges into consciousness only after extensive systematic reflection on the kind of specific rights appropriate to the social order. Nevertheless, basic rights and specific rights have inevitably qualified each other as elements in the same system from the very beginning. On the one hand, the personal and real rights which can be permitted to members of the society must be qualified by respect for the major interests of all the other members. On the other hand, the ways in which this respect can be expressed must be affected by particular individual and group relations. It is, indeed, in the course of trying to adjust special relations that men find themselves using the language of basic rights.

3. THE IDEA OF INALIENABLE NATURAL RIGHTS AND NATURAL JUSTICE

Some would press the conception of basic rights a stage further and argue for the existence of natural rights. Thus, according to the American Declaration of Independence in 1776 it is 'self-evident' that all men are created equal and endowed with certain inalienable rights including those of Life, Liberty and the pursuit of Happiness.

How far the colonists had reflected on the implications of this sweeping generalisation is not very clear. Judging by their own practices, negroes were not included in 'all men' and Life was not an inalienable right of King George's soldiers since they could be shot on sight.

Inalienable Rights. Are there any such rights? Is not this a contradiction in terms? 'Inalienable' means that a person cannot voluntarily divest himself of the thing; but the essence of a right is that it can be used, unused, retained or abandoned at will. In short, by its very nature, it is alienable.

Almost certainly the compilers of the Declaration were thinking, not of a person's inability to abandon his rights but of other persons' power or right to abrogate or withdraw them. But such a proposition is certainly not accepted in communities which, even if they reject capital punishment, admit the right to kill in self-defence. In such a case it is being declared that a person can forfeit his own right to life if he seriously threatens the life of another and is about to carry out the threat. We are not here concerned to agree with or dispute the proposition. We merely point out that 'inalienable right' is a contradiction in terms, and that the idea of a non-forfeitable right to life is rejected in many, probably all, civilised societies.

Natural Rights and Natural Justice. The conception of natural right has had a long history in political and legal theory; but it has varied so much in meaning that it can be effectively discussed only on the basis of some definite interpretation. In the present case we are concerned with the conception of natural right only in the sense of a number of specifically affirmed rights as, for example, in a declaration or charter of human rights. One of the great disadvantages of such charters is that they can be quoted in support of dis-putable claims, e.g. that the human dignity of a young tough who has beaten up and robbed an old woman is affronted by his being birched. The disadvan-tages are increased if adjudication on human rights is assigned to a special tribunal working exclusively in that rarified atmosphere.

These comments do not apply to the conception of natural justice. Super-ficially, natural rights and natural justice belong together; but natural rights are conceived as a collection of claims the validity of which is self-evident independently of positive law, while natural justice is an ideal employed in the day-to-day administration of positive law, supplementing existing rules or overriding *prima facie* relevant rules the application of which would be morally offensive. Natural justice is the ideal operative in the administration of positive law which identifies it as a system of norms within the moral order.

Can we say anything further about the conception of natural justice?

4. JUSTICE AND RESPECT FOR PERSONALITY

Let us look again at the American Declaration of Independence. The passage runs:

We hold these truths to be self-evident, that all men are created equal, that they are endowed by their Creator with certain unalienable Rights, that among these are Life, Liberty and the pursuit of Happiness. That to secure the rights, Governments are instituted among Men, deriving their just powers from the consent of the governed.

The rights singled out are to Life, Liberty and the pursuit of Happiness; but the formula has two fatal defects. The term 'right' is quite out of place, and for 'pursuit of Happiness' we must, as we shall see, substitute 'Property'. We are not talking of rights, but of the three fundamental conditions of the existence and enjoyment of rights. As a *living* being a person is a centre of intellect and will; with *liberty* he is capable of pursuing those values which have their source in his own nature; and possessed of *property* he can be the initiator and director of events in the material world.

The inclusion of Property as the third necessary condition of the existence of any system of rights requires some explanation. As a starting point we may refer back to the Introduction where it was asserted that a member of a moral order, as an active agent in the material world, must be an initiator, director and controller of events in that world. How he is by nature fitted for such control was explained in chapters Four and Five. Now, if a person is to initiate, direct and control events there must be some area in the material world within which *his* will and his will *alone* initiates and directs the course of events. Respect for his personality implies the acceptance by all other persons of his exclusive control within that area. This is the principle on which is founded the conception of a 'real' right as already defined and discussed. The most easily understood form of real right is property right, as e.g. landownership; and so I use the concept of Property for the area in which a person has exclusive control of the material world.

'Property' in this special sense does not imply any particular political, social or economic system; but it does signify a basic condition for the existence of a moral order, and hence a standard by which the practice of every political, social or economic order is to be judged. Exactly what area of autonomy should be assigned to the individual must depend on the general structure and resources of his society at any given time; and obviously there must always be some mixture of 'individual' and 'common' property. But the moral quality of any society must be judged by the importance it attaches to individual property, the external condition for the creative expression of personality.

It will be evident from the discussion in Part One on the foundations of the moral order that the being of whom we are now speaking is a person, a centre of self-directing activity, pursuing values which have their source in his own nature, modifying the pattern of these values in accordance with recognised norms and moulding the external world accordingly. Hence, when we give the so-called rights of Life, Liberty and Property their real meaning as the necessary conditions of personal exercise of rights, and when we say that governments are instituted for the 'securing of these rights', what we are affirming is that the ideal of justice, infusing the administration of positive law, is the securing of respect for personality. It is this ideal which identifies positive law as a normative system within the moral order; and what seems to be implied is that justice in this sense is the moral ideal itself.

In our next chapter we shall consider whether this is really so.

CHAPTER EIGHT

The Moral Ideal

In dealing with this part of our enquiry we cannot do better than follow—very broadly— the exposition of principles given by Kant in his *Groundwork of the Metaphysic of Morals*.[7] The book has some obvious disadvantages for the novice on account of considerable defects in the exposition. Although it belongs to his most mature years, he was still struggling with problems created by his earlier views, a struggle betrayed by the way in which the main trend of the argument is sometimes obscured or even diverted.

But all that being granted, it remains true that there is nothing in the whole of modern ethical theory comparable to the *Groundwork* for its insight into the proper approach to the theory of morals, for its grasp of the fundamental principles of moral judgement, and for its insistence on their being rooted in our rational nature.

In this chapter, therefore, we shall try to set out the essentials of Kant's elucidation of principles, ignoring defects of presentation, and shew how his philosophical analysis springs from his insight into the ordinary moral consciousness. To avoid any possible misunderstanding as to the relation between this exposition of Kant and the views of the present writer, I wish to make it plain that there is virtually a complete coincidence. To follow the development of his argument is the best way of presenting my own understanding of the principles of morals.

1. THE BASIC POSTULATE OF MORAL JUDGEMENT

Kant's aim, like ours, was to elucidate the principles operative in moral judgement, and his first care was to state what he believed to be most fundamental in ordinary moral thinking.* Its basic postulate, as understood by him, may be expressed in the following terms:

In assessing the *moral* quality of actions we attend, not to the specific end aimed at, nor to the success or failure in achieving it, but to the inner attitude of mind motivating the agent.

Is this really so? We often do evaluate actions in relation to their specific ends. We think it worth encouraging a man to get his car started if he is causing a traffic block. We also value success, rating a 'bull' on the rifle-range as higher than an 'inner' or 'magpie'. These points, however, are not in dispute. Of

---

* Kant's opening sentence is, in fact, 'It is impossible to conceive anything which can be taken as good without qualification except a good will', and this is often supposed to be the basic premiss of his ethical theory. It is, however, nothing other than a general value judgement *on* the good will and therefore irrelevant to the argument. Ethical theory is not concerned to evaluate the good will but to discover what it *is*. I therefore ignore the opening sentence and begin with the real opening of the argument, namely a statement of the psychological attitude to which (he believed) all moral judgement is directed.

course we value things in different ways, but the proposition is concerned with specifically *moral* valuation, and what it asserts is that moral assessment is on the inner attitude at the time of acting. This does seem to be the case. Suppose that, for some reason, a ship's captain has had his master's ticket withdrawn and that he cannot, on reinstatement, find employment. Eventually a shipowner offers him command of an oceangoing cargo vessel. How do we assess the shipowner's action? Initially we should all approve it as a humane step towards rehabilitation. But if we subsequently learn that the offer was motivated by the hope that the officer would later, out of gratitude, be a party to illegal transactions, we change our view. The action, judged by reference to its specific end and results is approved, for it confers a benefit on the man and his family; but the initially presumed moral quality is now denied.

2. NATURE OF THE MORALLY GOOD OR VIRTUOUS WILL
Proceeding from the postulate that the moral quality of an action pertains to the person's inner state of mind, we look for the attitude to which moral approval is given; and we find (1) that the morally good will is motivated by respect for duty, and (2) that this implies respect for the pure form of law.

(1) Respect for Duty
When investigating moral motives we ignore, of course, actions done in conscious opposition to what a person conceives to be his duty. But even if may action conforms to what duty requires, it may have been inspired by any one of three motifes. I may have conformed (i) as a means to some further end, or (ii) from direct liking for that kind of action, or (iii) because I knew the action to be a duty.

(i) This motive is clearly ruled out as the *moral* motive by the basic postulate of moral judgement. Driving at 50 mph, I see a sign '30' and decide to take a risk. Soon afterwards I see 'Police patrol in operation' and promptly reduce to 30 mph. I am now conforming to what duty requires; but it is clear that I obey the rule only as a means to an end—avoidance of being caught and fined. There is nothing wrong with conforming to the rule, but the motive for conformity has no moral worth.

(ii) But suppose that I actually like driving at 30 mph, prefering this leisurely rate unless circumstances dictate otherwise. I come to the '30' sign and keep to it as my maximum. But here, again, my conformity does not exhibit the morally good will if the *only* reason for conforming is that I happen to like doing that particular thing.

The conclusion in this case is not, at first sight, quite so compelling as in the case of (i). We may agree that to obey the rule of the road simply because one likes doing precisely what is in fact commanded is not the expression of a morally good will. But is the argument valid when our relations with people are concerned? It may be suggested that this second motive does sometimes express the morally good will in its purest form, performing acts of beneficence and charity, not from calculating self-interest, not from a sense of obligation, but from simple spontaneous affection for those concerned. Is not this what we mean by 'good will' *the* disposition which we morally approve?

As our purpose is to interpret the moral ideas of people in general, we must now go direct to ordinary experience for an answer to the question; and one thing is abundantly clear. Affection and all similar forms of good will play an essential part in creating and conserving a humane social life. It is difficult to imagine any reasonable person taking the contrary view.

But there is another side to the picture, one which suggests that we do not regard good will in this sense as the supreme manifestation of the moral attitude. And we shall understand why such good will receives only qualified approval if we bear in mind the psychological root of spontaneous affection. It and spontaneous antipathy are two aspects of one and the same mental trait. They are not inspired by the idea of some norm or principle. They are reactions to external situations—the physical and mental qualities of other persons and the circumstances in which the contacts occur. Responding to no normative ideas, but being merely *pro* and *con* reactions to fortuitous factual situations, the reactions will be themselves fortuitous. When performance of a duty is required, reliance on *mere* spontaneous affection for the person to whom it is due would be like relying on the assurance, 'O, yes. I know I ought to pay the grocer's bill, and I shall certainly do so if I ever come to like him personally'.

The difficulties arise not only with regard to the uncertainty of performance of known duty. Although affection is rightly valued as motivating kindly deeds, spontaneous affection can bestow kindness where least deserved while spontaneous antipathy has its way with the deserving.

In so far as the foregoing comments are a reasonably accurate reflection of the attitude of ordinarily thoughtful people, we can say that 'good will' in the sense of benevolent affection is not what they mean by the morally good will. It lacks the essential allegiance to some norm, ideal, rule or principle.

(iii) It is precisely this characteristic which we find in the remaining motive, namely doing a duty *because* it is a duty. The difference between it and the other two motives is fundamental. They express the desire for some particular state of affairs either as means or as end, while it is directed by a norm. That is to say, if I regard an action as my duty, do it because I so regard it, and would not have done it had I not so regarded it, then (it is considered) I am expressing the morally good will.

This does not deny the possibility of associated motives or collateral effects. Conformity to duty can be profitable. If a farmer makes a merely verbal agreement to supply the season's potatoes to an hotel for £x per cwt, this creates an obligation which may nonetheless be evaded for lack of proof. If the market price turns out to be higher than £x it will be unprofitable for the farmer to keep to the bargain. If he keeps to it because it has been made, we agree that his action is genuinely moral. If he would have kept to the bargain however the market rose or fell, and if it does in fact fall, his action will still be genuinely moral, but it will also be profitable. Why Kant sometimes seems to suggest the contrary is that, owing to the complexity of most practical situations, the moral motive is *manifestly* operative only when conformity is unprofitable.

(2) Respect for the Pure Form of Law
This second part of the argument is rather more intricate and is best taken in four stages to establish the propositions: (i) Acting from respect for duty means acting from respect for the *form* of duty; (ii) Respect for the form of duty means respect for law; (iii) Respect for law means respect for the *form* of law; and (iv) The form of law is its *universality*.

(i) We have established that the morally good will conforms to duty because it *is* duty. Now any act which is a duty has both form and content. The distinction between form and content is most easily seen in the material realm. A triangle, we say, is a plane surface bounded by three straight lines. It could be drawn on a blackboard, or cut out of wood, cardboard or cheese; but what makes it a triangle is its being bounded by three straight lines. Its *matter* is the material out of which it is made, while its *form* is its 'essential nature' to which we refer in defining it. Of course we never have pure form without matter, but the matter does not constitute the thing's essential nature. Squares and circles, as well as triangles, can be drawn on blackboards or cut from wood, cardboard or cheese, and it is 'being bounded by three straight lines' that differentiates the triangle from square or circle.

In like manner, a person's duty has both form and matter, the matter being the specific action to which he is directed, the form being that to which one refers in defining 'duty'. As the morally good will is motivated by respect for duty *qua* duty, this means that it is motivated by respect for the *form* of duty.

(ii) We define duty as an act or forbearance legally consequent upon the establishment of a right. It is an act prescribed by law. Hence respect for the form of duty means respect for *law*.

(iii) But respect for law is respect for the form of law. This must be so because we cannot accept the only possible alternative, namely that it is respect for the matter of the law, i.e. what the law happens to command in the particular case. Any rule or system of rules has some definite content—say the highway code or medical ethics. To be motivated by respect for the matter would mean to desire to bring *this* particular state of affairs into existence because it would be this state of affairs and not because it was prescribed by law. Hence, just as respect for duty means respect for the form of duty, so respect for law means respect for the *form* of law.

(iv) What, then, is the form of law? How do we define law? It is a formula or rule or system of rules of universal import. That is to say, the essence of law is its *universality*. This holds good whether we are talking of scientific laws of nature or of normative laws directing the conduct of rational beings. Thus, scientific law is of the form 'All A are B', as in a system of geometry or dynamics. Normative law differs from scientific in that it prescribes what ought to be rather than describes what actually is, but it is equally universal in form. Universality in form does not, of course, imply that a normative law regulates in the same manner the conduct of all human beings everywhere and in all possible circumstances. Universality consists in a defined class of persons being prescribed a certain course of action, the prescription applying to all without exception. 'Some people ought to take out television licences' is a mere generalisation; but 'All possessors of television sets shall take out television licences' is a universal.

To summarise the argument down to this point:

The moral judgement is the 'ultimate' or 'last word' judgement on the voluntary actions of rational beings. The principle governing that kind of judgement is therefore the supreme principle of Practical Reason. The judgement refers to the inner attitude or motivation of the agent, and the motivation of the morally good will is respect for duty which, on investigation, turns out be respect for the pure form of law, the form of law being its universality.

3. UNIVERSALITY: SUPREME CONCEPT OF PRACTICAL REASON

We began with what ordinarily thoughtful men mean by the moral quality of conduct. It is the attitude of 'dutiful' motivation. But we seem to have come a long way from the minds of down-to-earth practical men when we define this motivation as respect for the pure form of law (universality). This, it may be said, is an intellectual abstraction which can mean little to those immersed in practical affairs.

But nothing could be further from the truth. Provided that the steps in an argument are clearly set out, men in general are perfectly capable of following the logic, particularly when the whole process begins with a proposition they understand and accept. What we have done is simply to draw out the strict implications of the ordinarily accepted criterion of moral goodness. Formulated in philosophical terms, it is respect for the pure form of law, namely its universality.

That this formulation truly represents the attitude of down-to-earth practical people will be seen if we approach the matter from a different angle. Instead of asking 'What are you assessing when you pass a moral judgement?', let us ask, 'What do you regard as the ultimate test of right and wrong behaviour?'. To that question, if pressed to the extreme, the final answer is almost certain to be some form of what we call 'the golden rule'. In a naively savage way it is postulated in the children's rhyme,

> Tit for tat,
> Butter for fat,
> You kill my dog?
> I'll kill your cat!

On the same level a person will often justify his attitude by saying 'I paid him back in his own coin'. On a more constructive plane, there is the precept 'Do as you would be done by'. These are all negative or positive versions of 'the golden rule'; and its widespread acceptance down the ages is illustrated by the fact that when Jesus was challenged to say what he regarded as the greatest of the commandments he simply referred his interrogator to two passages in his people's sacred writ:[8]

Thou shalt love the Lord thy God with all thy heart and with all thy soul, and with all thy mind. This is the first and great commandment. And the second is like unto it, Thou shalt love thy neighbour as thyself.

On these two commandments hang all the Law and the Prophets.

For the non-theist this could be paraphrased, 'Give your absolute allegiance to what is noble, just and merciful; and translate that allegiance into practice by valuing your fellowmen as you value yourself. This is the wisdom of the ages.'

It is true that we have no way of proving that every person without exception does in fact accept the ultimacy of the golden rule. But the acceptance, explicit or implicit, is so general that the reasonable procedure will be to work out its implications. This is what Kant does, and what he finds is that it *must* be the universally applied criterion because it has its source in our rational nature.

The exposition consists in the expansion of two complementary propositions which Kant calls formulations of 'the Categorical Imperative'. This term is misleading because an imperative is a command or norm like the golden rule itself. What we are looking for is a principle which governs the kinds of imperative or norm which can claim moral validity. Let us, therefore, expound the argument in terms, not of an imperative but of a principle, subsequently shewing its source in our rational nature. The two propositions are. (1) The morally good will acts only on maxims it can will as law, i.e. will universally, and (2) The morally good will always respects persons *as* persons, never treating them merely as instrumental to its own ends.

(1) The Good Will as Respect for Law

When we say that the good will acts only on maxims it can will as law, this is what is called, for short, the test of universalisation. The test is so described because the form of law is its universality, and so, to will a maxim as law is to universalise it.

Two general points must be borne in mind at this stage of the argument. First, the test of universalisation applies, not to a proposed act but to the *maxim* of a proposed act. That is to say, the question is not 'Can I universalise lying?' but 'Can I universalise the maxim which in this particular case includes the act of lying?'. Much stock criticism of Kant is due to confusion between act and maxim, a confusion for which he himself must accept a large share of the blame. Second, the test of universalisation is a negative one. The proposition is not that the good will acts on every maxim that can be universalised. It is that the good will does *not* act on any maxim that *cannot* be universalised.

Let us now look at what is meant by a maxim, and what by 'willing a maxim as a law'.

Maxim. By a maxim is meant (i) a rule of action one proposes to follow (ii) to achieve a certain end (iii) in a given set of circumstances. For instance—to take Kant's own example—suppose that I am penniless and have exhausted the charity of my friends, but that a kindly stranger is willing to make a loan provided that I guarantee to repay it within a month. In order to get the money I propose to make the promise while knowing that I cannot possibly keep it. My maxim then is:

(i) I shall make a false promise
(ii) to get money
(iii) in circumstances such that it cannot be got otherwise.

Willing a Maxim as Law. Universalising a maxim or willing it as law means that one retains the *content* of the maxim but alters the *form* by substituting 'All men' for the purely personal 'I', and the normative 'may' or 'ought' for the factual expression of intention.

Thus,

THE MAXIM: *I propose to* make a false promise in order to get money in circumstances such that it cannot be got in any other way

on being universalised would become

THE LAW: *All men may or ought to* make false promises in order to get money in circumstances such that it cannot be got in any other way.

Maxim and universalisation thus understood, we have now to deal with two questions: (i) Under what conditions is it impossible to universalise a maxim? and (ii) Why, if it cannot be universalised, are we, morally speaking, prohibited from using it even as a personal maxim?

(i) The Possibility of Universalisation.

Since we are asking, not whether a maxim *ought* (or ought not) to be universalised but whether it *can* be universalised, the test is one of practicability. There is no doubt whatsoever that a maxim which includes the making of a false promise may be very effective for one's personal use. Would the use of a false promise to get money be good policy in the sense of achieving the end aimed at? The answer could well be 'Yes, indeed'. Here is a kindly old gentleman easily taken in by a pathetic tale and with a touching faith in the integrity of his fellows. He makes the loan; and so far, so good. But would there be any unfavourable longer-term effects? What would happen when payment fell due? It could be that prospects were still satisfactory. If the benefactor's character has been correctly read, there may be little to fear. Another tale of misfortune—the anticipated job has fallen through, or a dishonest partner has decamped with all the funds—might meet the situation. Indeed, if the story were sufficiently plausible, one might get, not only an extended period of grace but an actual cancellation of the debt. That being so, from the purely prudential point of view adoption of the maxim could be completely rational.

But would it be rational to attempt to universalise the maxim? Could one affirm the rule, 'All men may make false promises in order to get money when it is otherwise unobtainable'?

If this question is ever put as a live practical issue, we shall want to know all the relevant circumstances, including of course the grounds on which it was claimed that the money could be got in no other way. The following might be the type of case that would provoke reflection:

A nineteenth century millworker is caught in a period of mass unemployment. With a wife and three children, savings exhausted, no social security benefits, and facing the stark alternatives of either virtual starvation or securing money by fraudulent means, he chooses the latter course. Do we regard this act as justified in the sense of agreeing that any person so placed should be entitled so to act? Do we regard the maxim of the act ('I propose to get money by fraud in order to save my family from starvation in those circumstances in which fraud and starvation are the only alternatives') as universalisable, i.e. as a rule to be adopted by everyone in those circumstances with that end in view?

One might be called harsh and inhuman for saying No, but this would be to misunderstand the question. Humanity has nothing to do with the matter, for the question is not whether one *ought* to agree to the universalisation but whether one *can* do so. What has actually happened in the course of social and economic history is that, while declining to say Yes, men have acknowledged 'There, but for the grace of God, go I', have declined to accept the alternatives and demanded changes which would lessen and if possible remove the conditions giving rise to well-nigh irresistible temptation.

That, however, does not answer the question. If we cannot say Yes to the question of universalisation, when and why can we not do so? The short answer is that a person cannot universalise a maxim if the attempt to do so would involve him in a volitional self-contradiction. I give two examples in one of which the maxim could almost certainly not be universalised by anyone, while the maxim for the other could be universalised by many.

First, suppose I am a stockbroker and am sent a large sum by a group of clients to purchase a new issue offered by Auchenshuggle Goldmines Ltd. I agree; but as it happens, some heavy repairs have been done on an orphanage founded by me, and the builder is pressing for payment. I pay the client's money into my private account and settle with the builder, hoping that funds will soon accumulate to purchase the required shares. Can I universalise the maxim of my action in switching my clients' money to meet my private debt?

The maxim will be, 'I shall accept monies entrusted to me for a business transaction but apply them to meet a personal debt, hoping that a replacement will arrive in time to let me fulfil the obligation to my clients'. Can I universalise this and say 'All persons may accept monies entrusted to them for business transactions but apply them to meet personal debts, hoping that replacements will arrive in time to let them fulfil the obligations to their clients'?

I should, myself, be unable to universalise the maxim. It would confer on everyone the right to accept funds from *me* for one purpose and then divert them to a quite different purpose without my consent or knowledge, and without any certainty of timeous replacement. Now the planning of my life in accordance with my system of values—what is popularly called 'my pursuit of Happiness'—takes place within a social order guaranteeing my rights as well as determining my duties. Consequently, in 'pursuit of my Happiness' I necessarily will the conditions on which a successful pursuit must depend. But a rule which would entitle anyone, without my consent or knowledge, to ride roughshod over my rights and dispose of my property to suit his own ends would be absolutely incompatible with those conditions. It would therefore be impossible for me to will *both* the legal order governing the conditions essential to my achievement of Happiness *and* a rule of law completely incompatible with that legal order. It would involve a volitional self-contradiction impossible for a rational being.

It must be emphasised that the impossibility of universalisation does not arise from the falseness of my promise—my breach of faith in relation to my clients—taken by itself. It arises from the whole maxim of which that false promise is a part. There are possible maxims containing false promises which can be universalised. And this brings me to the other example.

Second, suppose that a close relative has been kidnapped by a criminal gang with the aim of extorting a large ransom. Word is sent to me that he will be released if I deposit the sum of £x,000 at a certain point at a certain time. I promise to deposit the money, but have absolutely no intention of doing so. With the aid of the police I make up a plausible package of dummies and arrange for an ambush. Of course there is a risk that the scheme may not succeed or that it may have tragic consequences; but the question we are asking is: Can my maxim be universalised? Can I accept that 'All men may make a false promise to secure the release of a relative held by a gang which the police have difficulty in bringing to book'?

For myself I should have no difficulty whatsoever in universalising the maxim. I should regard the false promise in that situation, and for that end, as the right of every man. It might not always be wise. If widely practised, one may expect criminal gangs to devise other means of securing ransoms, means requiring to be countered in other ways. But the question is not about the feasibility of the plan. It is a question as to the coherence of my own volitional attitudes. Can I will this law consistently with the maintenance of the conditions on which my life-pattern rests? If I can, then I can universalise the maxim.

(ii) Universalisation and Moral Judgement

Our first question was one of fact—When is it not possible to universalise the maxim of a proposed action? Our second question is not one of fact but of moral judgement: Why, if I cannot universalise the maxim, am I prohibited, morally speaking, from adopting it even as a personal maxim?

This is not a question which the moral philosopher can offer to answer in the sense of attempting to justify the prohibition. His task is not to assess the merits of 'the golden rule' but only to elicit and express its meaning in philosophical terms. In practical life the ultimate criterion of right and wrong is generally held to be the golden rule in some form or other, such as 'Do as you would be done by' or 'Do not that to another what you would not have done to yourself'. Translated into philosophical terms the golden rule becomes 'The good will acts only on maxims it can will as law'.

It is, however, the business of the philosopher, not to attempt to justify the use of this criterion but to look for its source. The source becomes clear when we note that the rule is affirming the supremacy of the concept of Universality, the form of law. Now the power of apprehending universals belongs to reason, and to reason alone. Hence if, as the golden rule affirms, acting conformably to universals is of the essence of morally right conduct, then the source of all moral standards lies in our nature as rational beings. The morally good will acts only on maxims it can will as law because this is the supreme expression of Practical Reason.

This conclusion must be interpreted with ordinary commonsense. We must not suppose that what is the right thing to do can be read off from the abstract formula, for the formula is only elicited from reflection on men's practical judgements and the reasons they give for them. Again, we cannot expect that seriously minded men will always agree on the maxims they would be prepared to universalise. Yet again, this account of moral judgement makes no claim that we should never proceed to act until we have applied the test of universalisation. It is very seldom that we have to appeal to first principles. What the argument does mean is that, if ever we have occasion to suspect the rightness of what we are about to do and squarely face the issue, this is the principle of 'last resort' which is applied.

(2) The Good Will As Respect for Personality

If Kant's analysis had ended with the proposition that the morally good will acts from respect for the pure form of law, it could never have been regarded as an adequate statement of the principle implied in the golden rule. There the emphasis is clearly on our relations with persons and not on our attitude to an abstract principle.

But this is precisely the emphasis in Kant's complementary formula. The good will always respects persons *as* persons, never treating them as merely instrumental to its own ends. That the two formulae necessarily go together is evident if we ask, What *is* law in the sense of a system of normative rules? Universality is of the essence of all laws, scientific and normative; but normative law is a system of universals governing the relations of persons. Hence respect for the pure form of normative or juridical law has its source in respect for persons universally. What in practice this means is explained in the preceding chapter. A person is a being capable of exercising rights and performing duties. The concept of 'right' has a priority inasmuch as duties are created in the creation of rights; and rights are opportunities for pursuing the good as envisaged by the individual. They are opportunities for the creative expression of personality.

CHAPTER NINE

Community

While Chapter Seven was concerned with positive law and Chapter Eight with the moral ideal, they are intimately related at the highest level, for the ideas of justice and respect for personality are common to both. But the relationship must be far more pervasive and intimate than merely on the plane of high principle. The moral ideal is revealed through the conscience of the individual member of the moral order who is at the same time a member of a community governed by positive law. Inevitably, therefore, the individual comes under two jurisdictions, under the judgement of the State court and under that of conscience. We want to see how far the two allegiances can be mutually supporting; and the topic as a whole can be covered in the following sections: 1. Positive Law and Moral Law, 2. State Court and Conscience, 3. Law-making Within the Moral Order.

1. POSITIVE LAW AND MORAL LAW

Despite the distinction often drawn between law and morality, morality, like positive law, has an essentially juridical character. The basic concepts—law, right, duty, obligation—are the same. Kant accepts the juridical character of morality, but he mistakenly identifies the ultimate principle, 'The good will acts only on maxims it can will as law', with 'the moral law'. Moral law is not a supreme principle. Like other forms of law it is a more or less systematic body of rules, even though in morality the systemisation is very rudimentary.

It is distinguished from positive law in the same way as any system of law is distinguished from others, namely by reference to the relevant judicial authority. The positive law of a given State is identified, not by references to the sum total of its rules at any given time, nor by references to their legislative sources, but by reference to the judicial authorities of that particular State. The positive law of England is the system of rules recognised and administered in the English courts. The positive law of Scotland is the system of rules applied in the Scottish courts. The law of the Church of England is the system of rules applied in its ecclesiastical courts, and the law of the Church of Scotland is the body of rules applied in the courts from Kirk Session up to General Assembly. By the same token, the moral law is the body of rules recognised and applied by the individual conscience—a term to be explained at a later stage.

The identification of moral law by reference to the judicial authority applying it avoids the fruitless attempt to distinguish it from other law by reference to a special content. The content, the rules recognised as relevant to any moral situation, can be traced to various sources. Primarily, there is the traditional behaviour pattern discussed in Chapter Two, and this will, of course, include an indefinite number of the rules of positive law. For the adherent of any religious denomination the moral law will embrace rules laid down by his communion, and so forth. All these rules are liable, at one time or another, to be considered relevant to the moral issues confronting the individual. Broadly speaking, the content of the moral law for any person will mainly coincide with the law of his State and of any particular associations to which he may belong.

2. STATE COURT AND CONSCIENCE

But while public court and private conscience are both concerned with the application of rules and principles, their approaches are very different. When determining what ought to be done in any given case, the function of the State court is to administer justice according to established law. Its first concern, therefore, is to ascertain the relevant established rules. These can only represent a consensus which may fall well below the most enlightened opinion; but such as they are they must be applied. This does not mean that courts are uninfluenced by questions of ultimate principle. On the contrary, principles are never entirely absent from their thought and there is at times an explicit appeal to natural justice. It remains true, however, that if there are clearly relevant and unambiguous rules, these must form the basis of the judgement.

The emphasis in conscience is quite different. While it would be impossible for anyone to make a conscientious decision completely uninfluenced by the customary standards of his community, the conscientious man does not begin by submitting those standards to systematic study in order to discover what he ought to do. He goes direct to the question, 'What in the last resort ought I to do?'. And while accepted rules will influence his answer, they are never decisive however relevant and clear they may be. The court works directly with rules which are governed in the long run by the idea of justice. Conscience looks directly to the idea of justice the actual appearance of which will always be coloured by contemporary law and custom.

(1) Relative Authority of State Court and Conscience

A further significant difference between State court and individual conscience is in their relative authority. The member of a community, as such, is necessarily subject to its government, as such; but this is a formal relationship. The government at any given time consists of individuals who may or may not meet the requirements of what a government should be and do. Allegiance to that particular group is therefore conditional, and each member of the community decides whether the conditions are being met. Naturally, the presumption is that the persons holding office are fulfilling their trust, but the presumption is not unchallengable. And since the matter concerns the allegiance of each individual member, it is for each individual member to decide whether the allegiance is due.

The authority of the government, and this includes the State court, is

therefore *conditional* for the individual member, while the authority of conscience is for him *absolute and unconditional*. It is unconditional, not only
with regard to matters on which he is recognised as the proper judge but also on
the question as to whether he shall obey the judgement of the court or
instruction of the executive.

The individual member thus comes under two jurisdictions, that of the State
court and that of conscience. The State court speaks for the community of
which he is a member while conscience speaks for himself alone. It may therefore be claimed that over-riding authority belongs to the State court. To reply
that conscience has authority to adjudicate on the propriety of obedience may
be met by the point that the judgement of a court can also be a completely
conscientious decision of the judge. In any case it is a plain fact that the sanc-
tioning power of the community is ranged behind the court. It is equally plain
that it would be a recipe for anarchy to demand that, in any case of conflict, the
State court should give way to the individual conscience. Indeed, the reflective
conscience would repudiate the demand since it is impossible to see how the
maxim of such a claim could be universalised. From the point of view of the
community, a decision of any one of its courts is not subject to over-ruling by
any individual conscience.

But from the point of view of the individual a judgement of conscience is not
subject to over-ruling by any court of the State. He may be compelled by over-
riding power to do what he believes to be wrong, but that is a very different
matter. External conditions, including the pronouncements of constituted
authorities, profoundly influence how a person thinks he ought to act, but the
operative factor is the personal decision. Threats, promises, and appeals to ideals
influence the formation of motives; but, a motive having been finally formed,
the consequent act is a response of 'the individual's own motion'. What he then
thinks he ought to do is a judgement which has already taken into account all the
external factors within his knowledge, amongst them being the imperatives and
sanctions pressed on his attention. The authority of State, church or any other
institution does not then furnish a judgement which *he* can consider as an
alternative 'ought', for the simple reason that his 'judgement of last resort', his
moral judgement, has already assessed their bearing on the issue.

The relative levels of authority in court and conscience can best be expressed
in the following way. Ultimate authority resides in conscience. When we say
that the authority of the public court, speaking for the community, *rightly*
over-rides the wills of its individual members, this right is accorded to the court
by the conscience of the individual who accepts the implied consequences of
rebellion. Authority is *ascribed* to the court as a matter of *right*, while supreme
authority is *exercised* by conscience as a matter of *fact*. When we assert the
ultimate supremacy of conscience, this is not a conclusion at which we arrive by
weighing its claims against those of other authorities; we are simply stating a
plain psychological fact. Conscience does not have a *right* to the last word; it
just *has* the last word.

It would be a complete misunderstanding to suppose that there is an inevitable conflict between State court and conscience. Such tensions as arise are not essentially different from those which occur between the consciences of different individuals. Court and conscience share a common aim and are complementary. Conscience can operate only in an organised society of which positive law is an essential condition; and opposition to governments which conform on the whole to the requirements of their office does not come mainly from profoundly conscientious people. On the contrary, the conscientious disposition—not to be confused with inflated egotism masquerading under the name—is the main source of social stability.

(2) The Nature of Conscience

To say that conscience does not have a right to the last word but just *has* it will, no doubt, suggest that we are adopting a 'command' theory of morals, arguing that right and wrong are simply what conscience tells us to do and refrain from doing. The suggestion is that, having rejected the 'command' theory in its theological setting, we are reviving it in an even less plausible form.

This is not so. As against the crude command theory, we found that the mature religious consciousness offers absolute and unconditional obedience only to a God in whom moral principles are conceived to be eternal, intrinsic attributes. His commands do not make right and wrong but express what, in any given situation, is required by the moral order.

It is on precisely the same grounds that we ascribe supreme moral authority to conscience. Its decisions do not make right and wrong but express what is required by the moral order. Its commands (so-called) are not dictates but judgements. In other words, the attributes assigned by the mature religious consciousness to its God are held by the mature moral consciousness to be attributes of rational nature as such.

That there should be this affinity between the conception of divine moral authority and the authority of conscience is not at all surprising, for it is a kinship frequently asserted in religious literature. According to *Genesis*, God created man in his own image, and St Paul makes the moral implication explicit:

When the Gentiles which have not the law, do by nature the things contained in the law, these, having not the law, are a law unto themselves; which shew the work of the law written in their hearts.[9]

In a similar vein we have the mediaeval theory of 'natural law' as a set of innate norms; and even the Reformation theologians, not very sympathetic to natural law theories, held that 'God created man . . . . after his own image, having the law of God written in his heart'.[10]

These theological ways of linking moral judgement and divine law are attempts to assign *origins*, but the philosopher's task is to say what conscience *is*; and Kant explains its nature and status in the following way:

Conscience is pure Practical Reason. This follows from the analysis of the morally good will as acting only on maxims it can will as law. Reason is the power (and the only power) capable of apprehending and acting conformably to universals. In its theoretical exercise it governs the procedures of pure and applied science. In its practical exercise it is operative through the valuational concepts of Utility, Economy, Integrity and Universality; and since moral judgement, operating under the concept of Universality, is the final judgement on any proposed plan of action, the activity of moral judgement is appropriately called that of pure Practical Reason.

3. LAW-MAKING WITHIN THE MORAL ORDER

(1) The Kingdom-of-Ends

From the identification of conscience with Practical Reason Kant draws a curiously expressed conclusion. This (he says) confers on the individual person the unique status of being 'both subject and sovereign in a Kingdom-of-Ends'. By the Kingdom-of-Ends he means an Ideal Community of Persons. The peculiar name used for such a community reflects a confusion between 'source of all values' and 'absolute value'. His argument, briefly, is this: All particular ends or objectives derive their value from their being desired by a self-conscious subject (The source of all value lies in the volitional nature of a person). Their value is therefore merely relative. They are ends, but only relatively so, i.e. they are desired only as means to fulfilling the desires of the subject. On the other hand, the subject, as the source of their value, is of absolute worth, an End-in-himself.

It is this equation of Person and End-in-Himself which Kant has in mind when he refers to the ideal community as a Kingdom-of-Ends (-in-themselves). He is confusing the notion of personality as the source of all values (which it is) with that of personality as of absolute value (which is not at all implied in being the source of values). But although Kingdom-of-Ends is a misnomer, the term is sufficiently striking to be retained, provided that we remember its real meaning.

Turning from the name to the substance of the concept, we note that moral judgement is concerned with inter-personal situations, with men in communities. Conscience reaches its decisions by applying the test of universalisation. Now the willing of a maxim as law is the willing of a universal in two senses: first in the sense in which every law is a universal, and secondly in the sense that the willing of a maxim as law is the willing of a law for all men. It is perfectly true that my willing of a law for all men is, in practice, only the method I use in order to discover what is morally right or wrong for me personally, and does not determine the right or duty of anyone else. Nonetheless, I accept the right or duty as held or owed by me only because I believe it to be properly held or owed by anyone else in the same situation. In a sense, therefore, my act of moral judgement, though actually binding on myself alone, is potentially valid for mankind as a whole.

How could this potentiality become an actuality? Suppose that every person in a community were omniscient, having infallible knowledge of all the needs of his fellows and of all relevant facts and future possibilities; then, when impartially affirming maxims as laws, each and every person would, of necessity, be willing precisely the same set of laws. The law for all would be freely willed by each; and so each would be sovereign in the community, and at the same time subject inasmuch as he would be unconditionally bound to obedience.

Of course men are not omniscient. Even if a person, having taken all reasonable care to ascertain the relevant facts, were completely disinterested in weighing the implications of his maxims, there would always be the possibility, nay the virtual certainty, that his assessment had been infected by ignorance. Consequently the content of his legislation would differ in some respects from that of other honest men. Hence, as Kant points out, the Kingdom-of-Ends is not and never can be an actual state of society. It is an ideal.

But it is not a mere ideal in the sense of having no practical relevance. It has relevance in two respects. First, its presence in the mind is a prerequisite of all moral judgement. In any moral context the individual must aspire to act *as if* he had perfect knowledge and a completely impartial will, even when well aware of his inevitable limitations in both respects. He has no alternative to acting on this 'as if' except the alternative of evading responsibility for taking a moral decision. As Kant puts it, the Kingdom-of-Ends is an ideal community into which we think ourselves when faced by the need to take moral decisions. And we can so project ourselves into the ideal community because conscience, the faculty of moral judgement, is Reason in its purest practical use, the power intrinsic to the nature of a rational being of apprehending and acting conformably to universals.

There is a second respect in which the moral ideal has relevance. The relation between positive law and morals has so far been considered in its judicial aspect. But in the conception of the Kingdom-of-Ends attention is centred on legislation, on an ideal community in which each and every member participates in making the law. How far can this be relevant to the making of positive law? In particular, is general participation possible; and can performance be assessed by reference to the Kantial ideal? These two questions will be considered in the next two sub-sections.

(2) The Sources of Positive Law and the General Will

As to law-making in general, the possibility of participation is intrinsic to our rational nature. Every person capable of making a moral judgement is capable of taking a decision in conformity with the golden rule, and therefore of affirming a rule valid for all persons in a given situation. Assuming an understanding of the interests and circumstances of the other persons belonging to a group of which he is a member, he is by nature capable of consulting with them and forming rules for the common good. Moreover, he will insist on having some influence on the development of the law. Any rules for common behaviour will limit the number and quality of the ends he can legitimately incorporate in his own system of values, and he will want a voice in determining what those limits shall be.

But granted the individual's intrinsic legislative ability and his justifiable interest in what laws are made, these do not necessarily ensure that he will participate in actual law-making. If he does participate, this will become apparent when we look at the generally recognised sources of positive law.

Sources of Positive Law. By sources we mean the origins to which a State court will point when accepting rules as belonging to the system it administers; and for well developed systems most or all of the following are recognised:[11] Judicial Precedent, Authoritative Writings, Equity, Custom and Legislative Enactment.

Judicial Precedent is a source in that when a court of appropriate status implicitly or explicitly rests its judgement on a rule not hitherto recognised, this rule will henceforth be accepted as part of the law. Obviously, the members of the community in general play no part here. *Authoritative Writings* are the works of learned jurists who profess to declare what the law is; and here again the members of the community in general play no part. *Equity*, like judicial precedent, is a source to which courts appeal in the actual administration of justice; and so it also lies outside the area in which members of the community in general could be contributors. We are thus left with Custom and Legislative Enactment.

Custom. We distinguish between custom as one of the sources of a modern legal system and custom which was virtually identical with the whole law of an ancient community. As a modern source, custom must satisfy a number of conditions, one of which is long-standing recognition by the people concerned; and it is a nice question whether the individual, as such, can be said to have participated in its development. Presumably no one said, 'Go to, let us make a custom'. Like Topsy, it 'just growed' and was given recognition when it had attained a substantial and well defined form.

It is more illuminating to consider custom in its wider form as folk law. In this wider sense, custom also 'just growed'. But how? We should begin by thinking of a small primitive community, either nomadic or in a village settlement, social organisation being determined by natural ties, authority vesting in the elders, heads of families and tribal chief or village headman. There the law evolved in the course of settling disputes. Initially, there would be no formal court. All that was necessary was a general meeting, e.g. a village assembly at which the plaintiff would state his claim or grievance and be answered by his opponent. This would be followed by general discussion until it appeared that a broadly acceptable view was emerging, whereupon a senior member, such as the headman, would pronounce the verdict.

Apparently, this procedure did not involve all the adult members of the community. Discussion of the case was properly confined to the older men, the women and the younger men being present as spectators. No doubt the urge to intervene at exciting moments could be irresistible, but it was definitely discouraged.

From this rudimentary method of dispensing justice evolved the body of folk law. A case having been decided, it would inevitably form an approximate precedent for the disposal of similar ones; and as broad rules accumulated, there would arise a need for their recording in the memory and consequently for recognised custodians who would transmit their lore from generation to generation and be the authoritative interpreters on any disputed point of law. Such jurisconsults were the *brehons* and *breeves* of Ireland and the West Highlands and Isles and the *lagmen* of Scandinavia.[12]

As the folk law developed, two factors operated to narrow the range of persons participating in the process. One was the mounting prestige of the custodians whose schools not only transmitted their learning but also sought to elaborate its rules. The elaboration was only partly occasioned by the need to deal with actual cases. It was also inspired by the attempt to work out a logical pattern to cover different types of hypothetical ones. Besides encouraging a lot of pedantic extravagance, this gave to legal development a strongly professional quality.

The other factor which largely excluded the general community from participation in lawmaking was the tendency for tribal kings to replace petty chiefs by royal officials and to supplement the common law by administrative orders.

In view of the above mentioned facts, it is clear from its origins in a judicial assembly and its elaboration by law school and royal order, that the customary law of an ancient community was made by persons with some special status and not by the community as a whole.

There is, however, another important fact to be borne in mind. It is that the law was not regarded as a set of commands imposed on the community. The verdict of the village 'court' was not imposed. It was a consensus of the wise men arrived at by open discussion for all to hear; and the body of law which emerged from such proceedings was the law of the folk, their law. True, it was generally said to have been given to them by some divine patron or heroic ancestor; but this itself opposed a considerable barrier to arbitrary rule. Chiefs and kings could ruthlessly exploit their people, but the law was sacrosanct, binding on all; and supernatural retribution, if not human revolt, was a hazard for the unjust judge or aspiring autocrat. This notion of government under law found practical expression in the periodical assembly which all freemen were qualified to attend. Partly fair and gala day, it was also the occasion for the hearing of important causes and passing royal ordinances compatible with the common law. Normally, they would have been presented with the consent of a council, and the approval of the assembly was, in the early stages at least, a condition of their validity.

So what we find in relation to customary or folk law is, briefly, this:

On the one hand, the community in general did not have any share in the making of the law. That was the prerogative of persons with some special status. On the other hand, the community had a degree of control over the lawmakers, over the lengths to which they could go in altering the traditional system. This control was based on the assumption of the sanctity of the law and the penalties of interference.

Legislation. While there is no clear historical dividing line between, on the one hand, the development of customary law through professional interpretation and royal order, and, on the other, development by legislation in the modern sense, there is a fundamental difference between the two conceptions. For the one, the common law is sacrosanct, the theory being that such rules as are made by kings and approved by assemblies are mere superimposed detail, leaving the main structure intact. But for the conception of legislation in our modern sense, the lawmaking powers of the State are limited only by the extent to which it recognises other independent authorities. Within its own sphere of legislative sovereignty there is no law beyond its power to amend or abrogate.

A necessary implication is that, with the downgrading of folk law and its supposed supernatural sanctions, the ancient safeguard against arbitrary rule has gone, and it is in face of this situation that political constitutions ranging from autocracy to democracy have come into being. We are concerned with these institutions solely with regard to the matter of legislation, and we have two questions to ask: *First*, do they increase general participation in the making of positive law? *Second*, are they any substitute for the ancient type of safe-guard against abitrary government?

As to the *first* question, the answer is that they make virtually no difference. The citizen of Great Britain has no more share in the making of positive law than had the ordinary member of the ancient village community. That is to say, *qua* ordinary citizen, he has none. The *second* question is the important one; and the answer here depends on the kind of constitution obtaining. In an autocracy the ancient safeguard is lost. In a democracy it is enhanced because of the influence which can be brought to bear on the legislators. That influence consists, first, in the right of full and unfettered discussion of public affairs. That right covers the advocacy of measures conceived as serving the common good, the exposing of bad laws and the recommending of good ones which should be enacted. It consists, secondly, in the power of the franchise to expel legislators who fail to respond and to replace them by others.

On the question of participating in lawmaking, then, the conclusions must be that Kant's ideal of a Kingdom-of-Ends in which each member is both subject and sovereign is inapplicable to the legislative process in a political community. Legislation is always performed by an authorised individual or group, irrespective of the nature of the political constitution. Where constitutions differ is in the power they give to the community over its legislators, both in the matter of opening up public issues for official attention and in the choice of persons most likely to respond.

(3) Assessment by Reference to the Kantian Ideal

The qualifications for acting as sovereign legislator in the Kingdom-of-Ends were omniscience with respect to all relevant present and future circumstances and absolute impartiality of the will. We saw that this is an operative ideal for the private conscience in the sense that the morally good will tries to fulfil the requirements so far as that is possible for fallible human nature.

It requires little argument to shew that precisely the same demand is made upon the makers of the positive law. This is, after all, the dominant normative system within the moral order; and both the public professions of lawmakers and the demands made upon them by members of the body politic imply that the legislators' performance is to be assessed by the Kantian ideal.

So much for the obligations laid upon the lawmakers. We do not hear so much about what is due from members of the community in general, but the standards are precisely the same. Democratic rights in the form of freedom of discussion and the franchise are the complementary sources of tremendous power. Separately they can be socially disruptive. 'One man one vote' for a people acquiring independence but unused to thinking in other than tribal terms readily leads to factional conflict and eventually to some form of dictatorship. On the other hand, a highly cultured and politically conscious people deprived of constitutional powers provides a rich seed-bed of revolution. But where the two sources of power are combined, uniting the ability to form massive public opinion with the influence to select the country's legislators, power there entails responsibility. Democratic right goes with democratic duty, and the members of a democratic State fall to be assessed as if they were in fact particpators in the legislative process. They are inevitably assessed by reference to the Kantian ideal.

That men are rational beings, capable by nature of using the golden rule as a criterion of behaviour, and open to social education through the public exploration of great issues, implies their ability to participate in the creation and maintenance of a moral order. It is true that a backward people may best be served by an enlightened aristocracy or autocracy, just as a man may be the better of using a crutch of sound timber. But the crutch will be abandoned when the man's weight can be borne by his own legs; and truly enlightened aristocracies and autocrats know that training for democracy must be the primary objective of their rule.

PART THREE

Corrective Justice

CHAPTER TEN

Reparation

The argument up to now has shewn that the moral order is created and sustained by the wills of its members in virtue of their nature as rational beings. But it is also liable to attack by those same wills in pursuit of personal and sectional interests; and the name 'corrective justice' is here used for the measures taken to repair damage and prevent its recurrence. As in the preceding chapters, we shall be dealing with both positive law and morals; and perhaps I should indicate once more that my approach is not that of a lawyer but of a moral philosopher enlisting jurisprudence in the service of ethics.

Corrective justice falls into two parts. On the one hand, there is the branch of civil law concerned with reparation and, on the other, the criminal law covering punishment in general. As it is in the latter field that the notion of responsibility is most in need of elucidation, we shall, in this present chapter, deal but briefly with the subject of reparation—very briefly because it poses only one main question for the moral philosopher, namely the question as to the principle on which persons are held liable to make reparation consequent on acts in breach of the law.

1. BASIS OF LIABILITY

Obligations under the civil law fall into various classes.[1] *Obligations ex Lege* are imposed by force of law, *Obligations ex Voluntate* arise from contract or unilateral promise, but the only class with which we are concerned in corrective justice is that of *Obligations ex Culpa*, i.e. those which arise from culpability, obligations binding on a person because he has done something for which he is at fault.

Thus, suppose A has borrowed B's motor-lawnmower, and that while it is in use the engine seizes up for want of oil. B demands reparation in the form of a new engine. Reparation has nothing to do with punishment. It is the restoration to an injured party of the enjoyment of a right or compensation for its loss. In some legal systems, including that of Scotland, reparation will be due only if the person from whom it is claimed was at fault. Was A at fault with regard to the damage to B's lawnmower? Had he been told that it was newly serviced and checked; or had he just assumed that it was all ready for use? Questions of this sort will be relevant to the imputation of fault; and if it is decided that there was fault on the part of A, he will be under an obligation to make reparation.

But when all the circumstances are taken into account, how is it decided whether A was in fact culpable?

2. THE REASONABLE MAN

Situations in which an obligation through fault will arise differ from country to country; but when we ask, 'What is the broad principle which determines the imputation of *culpa* and the consequent liability for reparation?', the answer is the same for English and Scots law, at least:

Culpability consists in conduct lacking in reasonable care, in doing or omitting to do something which, in all the circumstances of the case, would not have been done or omitted by a prudent and reasonable man.[2]

and

It is our duty to manifest that care and circumspection which may reasonably be expected of us in the circumstance. The measure [of culpability] is found in the answer to the question—How would a man of ordinary prudence and sagacity have acted in like circumstances; or rather in the circumstances as they must have appeared at the time to the person sought to be made liable?[3]

What this means is that, when a member of the community suffers loss unjustly and the aim is to secure redress, the procedure is to treat the wrongdoer as a reasonable man, to ask what a reasonable man would do in the situation, and oblige the wrongdoer to suffer the consequences of not having done so. The standard of behaviour is not defined by particular rules for particular cases. It is defined by reference to 'the reasonable man'. Of course he is not a model whose characteristics can be set out with precision, and not all judges would understand the concept in exactly the same way for a given case. But there are limits to the personal factor in interpretation. The reasonable man is not the same at seven years of age as he is at seventeen or forty-seven. The ordinary prudence and sagacity which we expect in advice as to where we should spend our convalescence after a certain illness is of a much higher standard for the doctor than for the travel agent; and for the advice on how to get there the standard is far more rigorous for the travel agent than for the doctor. But the criterion is in all cases the same. Anyone professing a certain craft, business or profession should have the requisite standard of competence. And any sane, mature person living in a community and enjoying its rights and liberties is implicitly professing the status of citizenship. He is therefore to be judged on the standards applicable to the good citizen, those which a reasonable member of the community would observe.

3. TWO MEANINGS OF RESPONSIBILITY

It will be observed that the reasonableness of the reasonable man is here a term of commendation. He acts prudently, responsibly, as distinguished from one who acts irresponsibly, rashly, carelessly, unreasonably. The one is to be commended, the other censured. But the associations reasonable/responsible, unreasonable/irresponsible have an entirely different significance when we are dealing with the criminal law, with crime and punishment. Irresponsibility of behaviour in the former context is a ground of culpability, while in the latter context irresponsibility excludes culpability. There is this difference in the significance of the terms because irresponsibility in the former sense refers to failure to meet the demands of a situation which the person was inherently *capable* of meeting, while in the latter sense it refers to an inherent inability to meet the demands. The person is irresponsible in that failure cannot be imputed to him as a wrongful act.

This latter distinction between responsible and irresponsible, between imputibility and non-imputibility, is of vital importance for the criminal law. If a person breaks the law, it obviously makes sense, before inflicting punishment, to ask whether it was possible for him to have done otherwise. If it was not possible, there would be no point in punishing him for the past action as a possible deterrent to a repetition of the offence. The question of responsibility is therefore of major importance in jurisprudence. It is no less important in ethics, and it will be the subject of our next chapter.

This is an account of *all* voluntary choice, whether non-moral or moral, whether of duty or of transgression; and if it be correct, then the statement (v) in the argument for free will is false. To say that choosing otherwise in precisely the same situation would have been possible is a contradiction in terms. It would not be self-contradictory to say that I might have chosen otherwise in precisely the same set of *actual* circumstances, for my assessment of them might have been different from what it was. The self-contradiction arises when it is said that the choice could have been different with the same *assessment* of the circumstances; for responsible choice *is* the volitional response required by a set of values and norms and by a certain assessment of the circumstances obtaining. Consequently there never can be a responsible voluntary choice which is other than the one made by the agent as so required. We may *behave* otherwise, but that would be irrational and irresponsible. To say, as champions of free will do say, that responsibility implies the power of *choosing* otherwise than one did, given a set of values and factual assessment, is a contradiction in terms because it is asserting the power to make a choice which is no choice at all.

From this it follows that '*ought* therefore *can*' as interpreted in the free will controversy is misleading. Starting off by surrendering to the determinist the whole of conduct other than the moral side, the effort to secure freedom for the residue omits to consider the very nature of a responsible act of will. For a correct understanding of moral responsibility we have to make a very different approach, starting from the basis of ordinary moral experience.

2. CULPABILITY AND VOLUNTARY CHOICE

Moral responsibility is peculiar in that the standards to which the individual should conform are discerned and authenticated only by himself, his conscience affirming what, for him, must be regarded as ultimately right and wrong. Bearing in mind that we are speaking of innocence and culpability as viewed by conscience, there will be general agreement on the following:

Unintentional departure from a standard is not considered culpable. Even though the departure may give rise to regret or even distress if the consequences are tragic, regret or distress for bad effects is not the same as remorse for faulty motive. Again, even when there is intentional departure from a known standard, there is no culpability if the standard is not already accepted as valid. There is a sense of culpability only if one is already committed to the standard which the present action dishonours.

But we have to pursue the implications of culpability rather further. When we remember the nature of voluntary choice it is evident that the real conflict cannot adequately be expressed as between a choice and a particular standard. Voluntary choice is the act 'required' by a certain set of values and assessment of the attendant circumstances. But when the act so required is contrary to the known duty, what we have is not the simple opposition of a wrongful act to a particular standard. The duty belongs to a known pattern of values differing in some respects from the pattern to which the wrongful choice belongs. That is to say, the opposition is between two value sub-systems, making for a cleavage within the volitional life of the person.

The sense of culpability indicates awareness of this cleavage. It also indicates that the valuational order to which the duty belongs—the one rejected—is in fact regarded as on a higher plane than the one actually chosen. It must mean this since the rejection is not approved but condemned. This reveals what is at first sight a curious situation. The voluntary choice is the one 'required' by the existing system of values and assessment of circumstances; and yet it is being condemned in the confession of culpability. How can this be?

The condemnation is explained by the fact that a person's choice at any given time is never (and never can be) made in the light of his whole system of values. It is geared to values of fairly immediate practical import and to circumstances which are fairly certain and not too distant in time. What values are of immediate import will, of course, vary with individual character and range of responsibilities. They will be different for a prime minister, a miner, a policeman and the owner of a betting business. But whatever the range of responsibilities, situations may suddenly erupt, calling for action with little time for reflection; and on these occasions a narrow set of values will dominate the view, leading to a choice which, almost as soon as made, may be repudiated as having been wrong.

It is further to be noted that, in feeling culpable, a person identifies himself with the order of values and norms his choice has rejected. This is of the very essence of the experience of remorse. It may relate to a major crime which has included cool planning, as in King David's seduction of Bathsheba and murder of her husband,[5] or a spontaneous reaction to a crisis; but whatever the occasion, remorse is an identification of the self with the moral order, inevitably so since it is the emotive side of a judgement of conscience. When David waxed royally indignant over Nathan's story of the plutocrat who had robbed a poor man of his one cherished possession, and was brought crashing to earth with '*Thou* art the man', he accepted the delineation of himself —'I am the protector and dispenser of justice for my people; and this is what I have done to two of them. *That* is the world to which I belong, not this one into which I have descended.'

3. CULPABILITY AND THE ALTERNATIVE CHOICE

The other proposition implied in the admission of culpability is 'I could have chosen otherwise'.

But is not this precisely the main premise of the argument for free will, 'I *ought* therefore I *can*'? Is there not a sheer contradiction between our account of choice as the required response in a particular situation and the proposition 'I could have chosen otherwise'? Doesn't the proposition mean that I could have chosen otherwise than I did in exactly one and the same situation?

No. 'I *ought* therefore I *can*' is being offered as a statement known to the logicians as an 'analytic proposition'. E.g., 'A triangle is a figure in space' is an analytic proposition because the idea of 'a figure in space' emerges in the analysis of the very meaning of 'triangle'; and what is being suggested is that '*Ought* therefore *can*' is a proposition of this kind, the 'can' emerging in the analysis of the very meaning of 'ought'.

We must, however, note that the statement 'A triangle is a figure in space' is an existential statement; it refers to the factual connexion between 'triangle' and 'space'. But can there be an analytic proposition in a normative context? Is it possible for 'can' to be included in the very meaning of 'ought'? What I morally ought to do (i.e. my duty) is determined by a judgement of conscience as to what is 'required' by the moral order. What I can do (what is possible for me)—meaning in the present discussion 'what I can choose to do'—is determined quite otherwise. A choice is the overt expression of a valuation, the acceptance of some thing or action as 'required' by a person's set of values and assessment of the factual situation. These two 'requirements' do not necessarily coincide. In the 16th century heresy hunts, a person might well accept that his moral duty was to confess the faith he held, knowing at the same time that this would be visited by a painful death. The alternatives would be (a) confess and be put to death, and (b) deny and survive. Which alternative he could actually choose would depend on what was 'required' by his system of values and assessment of his factual circumstances; and this might not coincide with his moral duty.

The position will be clearer if we distinguish between 'I could have chosen otherwise' and 'I can choose otherwise'. Since my actual choice was the one 'required' by the sub-system of values before my mind and my assessment of the circumstances, 'I could have chosen otherwise' cannot possibly mean that *with that set of values and assessment of circumstances in mind* I could have chosen otherwise than I did. It cannot mean that I could have made an irrational choice, one which was no choice at all. But it does have a meaning. It is the identification of myself with the moral order, the expression of an aspect of my will aspiring to live in conformity with that order.

It may be thought that this interpretation evades the whole question of punishment. If the proposition does not mean that I could have actually chosen to do right in precisely the same situation in which I chose to do wrong, if it is the case that my choice was the one required, does not this imply that I could not have been liable to punishment; and yet surely culpability *means* liability to punishment?

The answer is that punishment has nothing whatsoever to do with *moral* culpability. Moral culpability is discerned by conscience indicating disconformity to a standard to which the individual in question is self-committed. Punishment is inflicted by an external authority for the transgression of *its* standards. What is morally wrong and what is legally wrong coincide to a large extent, and indeed they reciprocate. Some things are made legally wrong because there is a consensus that they are morally wrong, and some things, such as paying my rates and taxes, I regard as morally right because they are pre-scribed by the positive law. But the non-payment of taxes will be punished because it is illegal, not because I regard it as immoral. It is one thing to say that legal and moral culpability coincide to a great extent because they are reciprocally influential. It is quite another to say that punishment can be asso-ciated with moral culpability. One condemned by his conscience may well feel obliged to make reparation to a person whom he has injured, and he will certainly want to avoid repeating the offence. He may somehow or other devise a penance for himself on the analogy of penance inflicted by his church. But punish himself in the real sense he cannot do, and no external authority can inflict punishment for what is purely a moral offence judged by his conscience to be such. The more one understands the nature and purpose of punishment the clearer does it become that it can have no connexion with moral culpability as such.

Having cleared away this superficially plausible objection, we repeat that 'I could have chosen otherwise' means, and in view of the nature of voluntary choice can only mean, an identification of myself with the moral order in the sense of aspiring to live in accordance with its standards.

From 'I could have chosen otherwise' we have distinguished 'I can choose otherwise'. This does refer to actual behaviour, but it refers to the future, not the past. 'I could have chosen otherwise' is what Simon, son of Jonas, thought when the crowing cock reminded him of his boast to be Simon Peter; and 'I can choose otherwise' is what Simon Peter thought when he finally left his nets. It is not a kind of private New Year resolution. It is a complete commital to use all the means necessary to carry the resolution into effect.

This is well brought out in a modest, but interesting survey[6] concerning a group of six persons resolved to attempt giving up smoking. Considerations of space preclude our going into details, but the following points emerged. Five of the six supported their resolution by adventitious aids—special filters, acu-puncture, pills, 'withdrawal clinics' and hypnosis. Of these five two were completely successful and others partly so. The sixth, relying wholly on willpower, succeeded without difficulty for some weeks, but confidently relaxing on one occasion, he fell victim. He considered that to resume the attempt would require a favourable set of circumstances. This means that all without exception, but to varying extents, felt that the resolution required buttressing measures. It should be added that one was aided by having a non-smoking spouse. A firm resolution was absolutely necessary. Lacking it, no props and aids would bring success; but with the resolution, aids of almost any kind helped. To explore the psychology of 'withdrawal' could be very rewarding but it lies outside our enquiry. The general conclusion to be drawn is that living up to one's ideals is not a matter of the exercise of free will. It is a matter partly of re-examining existing values and partly of adjusting external circumstances so as to ensure that the choice required by the value system and assessment of circumstances will be the one conforming to the ideal.

4. PERSONAL AUTONOMY

So far we have concentrated on the two main implications of the sense of culpability. But this approach yields no very clear idea of the nature of responsibility, and we shall now try a more direct approach.

'Responsibility' means primarily 'answerability', answerability or accountability to some person or body of persons for the fulfilment of a role, the meeting of certain obligations. Moral responsiblity means being answerable to the moral order that one should live up to the requirements of membership. In so far as a person fulfils this requirement he is said to act responsibly in a slightly different sense, 'behaving responsibly' being a term of commendation; but it is the primary sense of answerability with which we are concerned. Two questions at once arise: What are the demands made on a member of the moral order? What makes it possible for him to fulfil them?

The answer to the first is that membership requires each to respect all the others as persons. To the second question the answer is equally straightforward. The ability to meet the requirements is an intrinsic attribute of rational nature: it is the capacity to apprehend and act conformably to universals.

But while conformity to the requirements of the moral order is a rational activity, so is transgression of those requirements. It is condemned as culpable; but only a voluntary action can be culpable; a voluntary action is an overt expression of a valuation; and valuation is governed by rational concepts.

Now since both conformity to and transgression of the standards of the moral order are rational, there must be different degrees of rational behaviour; and reflection shews that the difference between moral conformity and transgression derives from the different concepts in accordance with which choices are made. We have a somewhat similar distinction between adequate and inadequate performance in the non-moral realm. Someone is instructed to buy half-a-dozen chairs for the diningroom, and he comes back with 2 kitchen chairs, 1 office desk-chair, 2 from a suite of some sort and 1 from a sale of ship's furniture. He reports that they are all thoroughly sound and serviceable; but however true this may be, he has behaved very stupidly. His choice has been quite rational according to the concept of Utility, but any reasonably intelligent person would also have employed the concept of Integrity. What was required was a diningroom-suite, not a mere collection of things to sit on.

In a moral context culpability derives from failure to take into account the inter-personal dimension. Thus, following a rumour of food scarcity there may be a wave of panic buying. It is a perfectly rational reaction within its own limits. Bulk buying and hoarding are sensible measures to counter a threatened shortage. But one man's hoarding can be another man's deprivation. To the extent that this is so the reaction is culpable. It is a very restricted form of rational conduct, the concept of Universality (which is specially relevant to the situation) having been inoperative in this case.

While, in explaining the nature of responsibilty, conformity to the requirements of the moral order can be described without much difficulty, the same does not hold with respect to transgression. There is a curiously complex psychological situation. We are dealing with an individual person, a unitary centre of intellect and will, one in whom we discern the spiritual attribute of Selfhood; but this unitary nature is manifest in conflicting ways. First, there is conscience, pure Practical Reason without which we could not meaningfully speak of either moral conformity or transgression. Then we have the immoral choice with its sub-system of values and, opposed to it, the sub-system of values directed towards conformity. Conscience ranges itself with the latter side of this divided will; and it might therefore be assumed that culpability is attributed exclusively to the former.

This assumption would be entirely at variance with the facts of experience. Culpability is attributed to the will as a whole because the moral agent is an autonomous person—a self-directing centre of intellect and will, a self-governing rational being. There are not two wills; there is one will in a state of disintegrity. The volitional aspiration towards conformity shares in the culpability because it has not overcome the influences which made the immoral choice the required response. It is the will as a whole which is held to be responsible for conforming, and the will as a whole is culpable in so far as it has failed. Conscience is the self at its highest level passing judgement on itself as a whole.

It is important, however, to distinguish between responsibility and culpability. Morally speaking, there are no degrees of responsibility. A person just is responsible or answerable for his conduct, good or bad, *qua* moral agent. But there are degrees of culpability; and they are measured, not by the extent to which a person achieves or falls short of conformity, but by the extent to which the will to conformity has been more than a pious resolution. Conformity being the end, relative culpability is measured by the extent to which that end has been purposefully sought. Genuine striving involves the review of detailed values and adjustment of external circumstances with a view to the 'required' choice in a given situation becoming the one required by the moral order.

To bring the whole discussion into focus, we may conclude by saying in a few words what moral responsibility is and what is its practical significance. Moral responsibility is the potentiality inherent in an autonomous personality of conformity to the standards of the moral order. We say 'autonomous (self-governing) personality' because the standards of the moral order (the laws of the Kingdom-of-Ends) are willed and maintained by its members. They are willed in accordance with Practical Reason in its highest manifestation under the concept of Universality. The potentiality of conforming derives from the fact that this same Practical Reason, operating through the whole range of concepts from Utility to Universality, gives form to our systems of value, the systems in accordance with which our day-to-day choices are made.

The practical significance is that this potentiality inherent in our nature makes it impossible to set limits to the growth of any individual's moral stature. We are, of course, talking of potentialities, not certainties. We know that crime and delinquency will always be with us. But we cannot know which, if any, of the existing criminals and delinquents will always be so. Moral answerability, as an intrinsic attribute of rational nature, implies a potentiality of which every rational being can become aware, and this awareness is the foundation upon which all development towards moral maturity must build.

CHAPTER TWELVE

Crime and Punishment

We shall now consider how far this account of moral responsibility is reflected in criminal law. This is a very limited enquiry within a vast field; but the discussion can be kept within manageable limits if we restrict ourselves to two main questions: first, How far does the conception of legal responsibility corresponds pond to that of moral responsibilty as already expounded? Second, How far do the measures adopted for the prevention of wrongdoing fit in with our conception of the nature of voluntary activity?

1. RESPONSIBILITY IN POSITIVE LAW

(1) Implies Rationality

Responsibility in Positive Law is essentially the same as moral responsibility in the sense that responsibility implies rationality. Thus, Thomas Erskine:[7]

It is agreed by all jurists, and is established by the laws of this and every other country that it is THE REASON OF MAN which makes him accountable for his actions, and that the deprivation of reason acquits him of crime.

One of the best known definitions of responsibility is contained in the McNaghtan Rules. In 1843 McNaghtan was acquitted on a charge of murder on the grounds of insanity. As the victim had been the secretary of Peel (in mistake for Peel himself), the acquittal aroused a good deal of public debate, and the Law Lords were invited to report on what they believed to be the law of England on criminal responsibility. From their report, we take the two clauses most germane to our enquiry:[8]

1. Everyone is presumed sane until the contrary is proved.
2. It is a defence to a criminal prosecution for the accused to shew that he was labouring under such a defect of reason, due to disease of the mind, as either (a) not to know the nature and quality of his act, or (b) if he did know this, not to know that he was doing wrong.

While the terms of the second clause have been much criticised (e.g. in the *Report of the Royal Commission on Capital Punishment* (Cmd 8932 HMSO 1955) especially pars. 226–250), the main objection being that it accepts too narrow a definition of mental disease, these are objections on points of detail. What concerns us is that criminal responsibility is firmly associated with un-impaired reason and irresponsibility with some 'disease of the mind', some 'defect of reason', making the person unable to grasp the relevant facts, especially the nature and quality of his act and its relation to a rule of law.

This view is put more fully in Hume:[9]

If (a person) cannot distinguish a friend from an enemy, or a benefit from an injury, but conceives everything about him to be the reverse of what it really is, and mistakes the illusion of his fancy in that respect for realities . . . his judgement of right and wrong is, as to the question of responsibility, truly the same as none at all.

(2) Irresponsibility

It is, however, one thing to have agreement on the comprehensive proposition that criminal responsibility implies healthy reason and irresponsibility implies defective reason, but quite a different matter when we ask just what constitutes defective reason. We may say 'insanity'; but what is insanity? Do we accept the conception of irresistible impulse? These questions, and many like them, are for the medical and legal professions to ponder; but it is possible to reach a broad definition of what constitutes irresponsibility by looking at the kinds of mental state which are regarded as good defences to a criminal charge, and then asking what sort of defect or defects of reason they betoken.

One ground of irresponsibility is the inability to know an action to be wrong; i.e. the inability to apprehend a rule (a universal) and to see whether an action falls under it. Further, a person might have this knowledge and yet be unable to conform.

A person is not responsible for criminal conduct if at the time of such conduct as a result of mental disease . . . he lacks substantial capacity either to appreciate the criminality of his conduct or to conform his conduct to the requirements of the law. (*American Model Penal Code*)[10]

The defect of reason here in question is *the inability to apprehend and act conformably to universals*. This certainly is a ground of irresponsibility in both positive law and morals.

Another ground specially mentioned by Hume is the inability to comprehend the true facts of a situation. This covers the 'McNaghtan' reference to inability to know the nature and quality of the act performed, but it has a much broader significance, covering, e.g., delusions about oneself. If a person were to say, 'I am Wellington, victor of Waterloo', and could shew the theatrical bill and the programme with his name opposite that role, he would be verifying his statement by putting it in an objective context. But he might well be claiming, not the dramatic role but to have actually fought the battle. For this there could be no verification and the impossibility could be demonstrated to him. But if he continued to make the claim he would be revealing a defect of reason, namely *the inability to verify the truth or falsity of a belief*. This, again, would be regarded by both positive law and morals as a ground of irresponsibility.

We have now the basic definition of criminal irresponsibility. It is *the inability through defect of reason to apprehend and act conformably to universals or to verify the truth or falsity of a belief*. Thus far, responsibility and irresponsibility in positive law mean the same thing as in morals. Court and conscience may take very different views as to whether a given person in given circumstances was responsible for his action; but fundamentally they are talking about the same thing, the health or impairment of his rational powers.

Various topics bearing on responsibility have an ethical relevance; and amongst the most important are 'diminished responsibility', 'irresistible impulse', and actions under 'necessity', 'coercion' or 'superior orders'.[11]

(3) Diminished Responsibility

Ordinary experience suggests that there is no firm line which can be drawn between complete responsibility and complete irresponsibility. They shade into each other; and it is best to begin with the idea of full rationality—not indeed the perfection of theoretical and practical wisdom, but that of 'the reasonable man'—and to think of gradually diminishing competence until a level is reached at which it is realistic to speak of irresponsibility rather than of a low degree of responsibility. The point at which a person is placed on this scale is a matter for professional judgement; but the idea of levels of rationality, and therefore of responsibility, would seem to be appropriate.

While this statement of the position would seem to have the support of most legal systems comparable to our own,[12] it has been challenged. 'Diminished responsibility', it has been argued, is not a legitimate concept of positive law. Thus, Lord Johnston:[13]

I can understand limited liability in the case of civil obligation, but I cannot understand limited responsibility for a criminal act. I can understand irresponsibility, but I cannot understand limited responsibility—responsibility which is yet an inferior grade of responsibility.

and L. J-G. Normand:

The defence of impaired responsibility is somewhat inconsistent with the basic doctrine of our criminal law that a man, if sane, is responsible for his acts and, if not sane, is not responsible.

It may be thought that these objections fail to distinguish two questions we need to ask about responsibility: *first*, Had the person powers of reason adequate to distinguish right from wrong and to respond to incentives to act rightly? The answer must be a straight Yes or No. *Second*, if the answer is Yes, how far did his mental powers rise above the minimal requirements? The answer in this case could be in degrees of rationality/responsibility.

Is there not a good analogy? Candidates sit an examination with a pass requirement of, say, 60%. At 60% you pass; below it you fail; there is nothing in between pass and fail. But you can score 70%, 80%, 99%. While pass and fail are exhaustive alternatives, there can be higher and lower degrees of passing.

So, it may be urged, with criminal responsibility. Rational powers can vary enormously. They can fall to a point at which a person is unable to understand and conform to the law. Above that point he is responsible and below it he is not. The alternatives are exhaustive. And this, presumably, is what Lord Johnston and L. J-G. Normand had in mind. But a person's mental powers may be well above the minimal requirements for responsibility or they may be less robust. Does it not follow that degrees of responsibility will go along with variations in rational powers?

However, if we are looking for legal and moral parallels, the suggested analogy oversimplifies the issue. As we have seen in the preceding chapter, the idea of 'degrees of responsibility' can have no place in a moral context. There we distinguished between responsibility and culpability. Responsibility is an intrinsic attribute of rational nature, the power to answer or measure up to the demands of the moral order. This means the ability to apprehend universals and what falls under them in given contexts, i.e. to make moral judgements. To make such a judgement, one thinks oneself into the Kingdom-of-Ends as both sovereign and subject, and judges *as if* one were perfectly impartial and perfectly cognisant of all the relevant considerations, as if one's capacity to answer the demands of the moral order were complete. Does this 'as if' correspond to the reality? To ask this question in a moral context is meaningless because the person about whom it would be asked and the person who would ask and answer it would be one and the same person—the person who affirms the 'as if' as a necessary condition of making the moral judgement. If one does not have moral responsibility one is incapable of making a moral judgement. If one makes a moral judgement one postulates complete responsibility.

Culpability is a quite different matter. It is concerned not only with the power of making moral judgements but also with the ability to put them into effect—an ability limited by psychological, physiological and environmental conditions. Culpability varies, not according to degree of success or failure but according to the degree to which one has used all available resources to put the judgement into effect; and the individual concerned, knowing the extent of the effort, can attach a meaning to the conception of degree of culpability.

How far does the position in positive law correspond to that in morals?[14] So far as culpability is concerned, there is a real parallel. A poor man stealing food for his starving family is responsible, answerable before the law, and guilty of theft. But his punishment in a humane society will be mitigated because of the circumstances. It will be accepted that there is diminished culpability in his theft as compared with theft by a man who is comfortably off and motivated by greed. The concept of diminished culpability is significant in positive law, just as in a moral context the culpability of the alcoholic who spends too much on drink is affected by the determination with which he has tried to resist the temptation.

But what of 'diminished responsibility'? When this question is discussed, the cases cited are very different from those relating to culpability, i.e. from those in which a person of sound mind has succumbed to temptation (e.g. the theft of a starving man). They relate to defects of reason, the most serious of which might be classified under 'insanity'. Here, quite clearly, we are dealing with diminishing degrees of rationality; and since rationality and responsibility go together, surely it is proper to speak of diminishing degrees of responsibility.

In positive law, then, penalties can be adjusted either to degrees of culpability or to degrees of responsibility.

It may be suggested that the conception of diminished responsibility must be as applicable to morals as to positive law. If a person's powers of apprehending rules of law are impaired, surely this defect of reason will extend to the making of moral judgements. Yes, that is so; but we must avoid confusing two different questions:

(i) To what degree has a person the ability to make responsible moral judgements? The answer is, To the same degree as he is able to understand and conform to positive law. Here the question is raised and the answer given by an external observer. (ii) What self-responsibility (in the sense of rationality) do I postulate in making a moral judgement? The answer is 'Perfect responsibility' since, in making a moral judgement, I think myself into membership of the Kingdom-of-Ends. A person might be able to agree that, objectively, his ability to make moral judgements is not of this high order. Indeed, ordinary common-sense would compel such an agreement from everyone who considered the matter. But however diffident one might be about one's competence to make a moral judgement on a particular issue, if he were brought to the point of making it, he would, of necessity, do so 'as if' his impartiality and cognisance of the facts were perfect.

We may now state, as simply as possible, our conclusions as to whether the idea of 'diminished responsibility' is valid and common to both positive law and morals. It is valid and common to both in that a defect of reason must involve a diminution in the power to understand and practically apply positive law and a corresponding diminution in the power to make sound moral judgements. What tends to obscure this common ground is the fact that, in making a moral judgement, a person necessarily discounts the possibility of fallibility.

Note. In the matter of adjustment of penalties, it would seem *prima facie* that, since strong temptation or low mental ability will carry less sensitivity to the legal requirements of a particular situation, the sanctions to secure conformity should be proportionately heavier. In fact the reverse is the case, and for a very good reason. Sanctions against the guilty are addressed to the will. For a person of superior rational powers, well aware of his place in the normative order and the significance of its demands, and under no strong temptation, wrongdoing is not a clumsy or desperate expedient. It exhibits a degree of indifference to or even contempt for the law, meriting an appropriately high penalty. 'Diminished responsibility', therefore, is not merely an intelligible concept. It is one which is necessary for the just administration of the criminal law.

(4) Irresistible Impulse

The attitude to this concept is rather indeterminate and it is apt to be discussed in general terms in connexion with insanity.[15] Here, without special reference to actual criminal conduct, we shall simply try to clarify the meaning.

(i) Irresistible Impulse and Voluntary Choice. Some responses to situations may be initially impulsive but capable of being brought under the control of the will. Thus, if a person has to undergo medical treatment involving a series of hypodermic injections, it is very common for the first response to be irresistibly impulsive, an immediate shrinking from the unanticipated stab of pain. It is involuntary because, while the person is aware of the shrinking and aware that it is a shrinking from the pain, the evasive action has not been envisaged before it actually takes place. But the first experience having been endured, a person can set himself to resist, and actually succeed in resisting the withdrawal impulse on subsequent occasions. He begins with an irresistible impulse and passes on to voluntary resistance.

Rather different but coming under the same general heading are cases of smoking, drinking and drug-taking. The habit having been acquired, physiological conditions develop which result in a craving for its continuance; and so we get the confirmed smoker, alcoholic and drug-addict. The impulse to smoke, drink or administer the drug can be irresistible in the sense that, on a given occasion, one is powerless to resist even if one would like to do so. But all these addictions may be overcome if the will is resolutely set to master them, and if one searches out and makes use of such means as will assist the resolution. This is the point of theoretical interest in the survey already noted of efforts to stop smoking. It is true that many people, especially among alcoholics and drug-addicts, never succeed. But unless they have some mental defect, the lack of success is due to a lack of will to succeed. This is not a criticism but plain statement of fact. It is quite possible to decide that since the effort is so costly in many respects, it should be abandoned. But this is a voluntary choice, the required response to a system of values and assessment of the relevant situation. Still, the fact that people do think it worth trying confirms our analysis. These addictions belong to the class of response which, though irresistible on particular occasions, may be permanently resisted by one who, steadily willing the end, wills also the known indispensible means. Conquest of the addiction may be merely an aspiration never fulfilled, but the fact of its being an aspiration at all puts the impulsive action into the category of responsible rather than irresponsible behaviour.

In the same category we should place the impulse to flee from a sudden, unexpected danger or to retaliate against an unexpected blow. Soldiers and policemen train themselves not to flee, and saints are disciplined to resist impulsive retaliation.

(ii) Impulse Beyond Voluntary Control. When speaking of impulses, initially irresistible, as brought under control by the will through the use of counteracting measures, we are not speaking of some special faculty called 'free will'. The reference is to the ordinary process of voluntary choice. The idea of giving way to the impulse is set in the context of a system of accepted values, and it is repudiated as incompatible with the main constituents of that system. E.g. the impulse to drink may be set over against a system of values which includes business prosperity and family security.

This means that the ability to bring a hitherto irresistible impulse under control is dependent on the power of reason to view that potential response in the light of a system of values and an assessed set of circumstances. Where that power of reason is lacking, it will be impossible to control the impulse, since its rejection cannot be made the objective of an act of voluntary choice. Whether such a condition of the mind is called insanity or by some other name is immaterial. The essential point is that it is a form of irresponsibility, a condition of the mind from which may issue behaviour which is not the expression of voluntary choice.

It will be understood that the existence of irresistible impulse in an absolute sense is not being here asserted. The point is simply that, if a person is subject to impulses which are irresistible, this can only be due to a defect of reason, namely the inability to foresee the impulsive action as a possibility and view it in the context of a given system of values and assessment of circumstances. Should there be such an inability, there could be no act of choice either to release or to inhibit the impulse.

5. Necessity, Coercion and Superior Orders

Although Diminished Responsibility, Irresistible Impulse, Necessity, Coercion and Superior Orders are all relevant to the question of penal liability, the notions of Diminished Responsibility and Irresistible Impulse are concerned with the nature of voluntary choice, responsibility itself, while Necessity, Coercion and Superior Orders are objective facts pertaining to the circumstances in which voluntary choice takes place. They lie, therefore, on the periphery of moral theory.

(1) Necessity and Coercion.[16] The common characteristic is that in both cases a person is faced by an enforced choice between alternative lines of conduct, one of which imperils his life or property, the other being a *prima facie* criminal act. The concept of *Necessity* applies where the confrontation of the alternatives is not willed by any person, where, e.g. a man preserves his house against an advancing forest fire by burning a neighbour's plantation to constitute a fire-break. The enforced choice between losing the house and the act of fire-raising is neither willed nor preventable by anyone. The concept of *Coercion* applies where the confrontation is deliberately willed, as when a car-owner is ordered at pistol-point to take a time-bomb to a busy market-place. The confrontation of probable loss of life with the alternative of delivering the time-bomb is deliberately created by the terrorist.

There is, therefore, no great difficulty in understanding the nature of action under the stress of Necessity or Coercion. The difficulties arise when we ask what should be done about the man who commits the *prima facie* crime of fire-raising or depositing a time-bomb in the market-place. Are necessity and coercion good defences against a criminal charge, or do they only merit sympathetic treatment in the matter of sentence? On such questions of conflict between duty and interest the moral philosopher has, as such, nothing to say. They are questions of legal and moral judgement on specific cases, directed to the man of informed practical wisdom; and we find that judges do not all agree on the legal answer, nor do all men of enlightened conscience agree on the moral answer. It is, however, significant to note an increasingly firm consensus that action in defence of life or limb is on a different level from action in defence of property, respect for personality coming before care for any particular right.

(2) Superior Orders.[17] Here we are concerned, not with a conflict of duty and interest but with a conflict of legal duties. On the question of liability for a crime committed under superior orders, the position in English and Scots law seems to be that a distinction is drawn between the liability of a servant under a private master and the liability of someone under a chain of authorities deriving from the State. The order of a master to his servant is not generally regarded as a defence to a criminal charge; but the position of one acting under State authority can best be illustrated in the case of a member of the armed forces. Here we are dealing with a case of conflicting *prima facie* duties under positive law. If a soldier is ordered by his platoon commander to commit a crime, both the performance of the act and the refusal to perform are, *prima facie*, criminal offences since a soldier is bound to obedience under military law.

Suppose, then, that the soldier obeys the order and thus commits a criminal act. Is he in fact guilty of a crime? The answer seems to be that he is not guilty and that the superior order is a good defence *unless* the action commanded is so flagrantly illegal or morally corrupt that he could not be unaware of its character. The *prima facie* duty of instant obedience takes preference over the duty to assess the broader legality of the action, but the priority is not absolute. This generalisation may need some qualification, but it seems to be sufficiently accurate for our purposes.

Is this answer satisfactory from the ethical point of view? There are three possibilities: unqualified liability, unqualified immunity, qualified immunity. That there should be at least qualified immunity seems reasonable. If you have a general system of criminal law, and if you then create an organisation such as an army to maintain internal order and national defence, an organisation which can be effective only if it is rigidly disciplined to operate through a hierarchy of commands; then, willing this organisation, as an end, you necessarily will the known indispensible means, namely the instant obedience of any member to the authority immediately above him. At the very heart of the organisation, therefore, is the power to create a conflict of legal duties, duties flowing from the criminal law in general and duties following from the essential nature of the organisation. And since the command of the immediate superior is by far the most unambiguous, and the general criminal law somewhat remote, reason gives priority to the immediately superior authority. Consequently it would be irrational to attribute unqualified liability for infringement of the general criminal law when that is done as the performance of the most obvious legal duty.

That being so, should not the immunity be unqualified? No. The conflict of *prima facie* duties is certainly a conflict within positive law; but the positive law is a normative system within the moral order as a whole, and in the last resort the individual is thrown back upon the authority of conscience. In some cases the decision of conscience will be clearly against the immediate authority, and there would therefore be moral culpability in obedience. At the same time, disobedience might be visited by immediate death, and conscience might not regard obedience as culpable if that were a serious threat. It could be that liability for breach of the general criminal law would be minimal unless the act to be undertaken were so revoltingly contrary to the dictates of humanity that the risks inherent in disobedience must be accepted.

This is the position recognised in practice. The legal and moral duty is instant obedience to the immediate superior unless the act commanded is flagrantly at odds with general legal duty, in which case the over-riding duty is to disobey. While obedience would not be guiltless, it would carry qualified immunity.

What is true of the private soldier's duty of obedience to his platoon commander is true of every ascending rank up to that of commander-in-chief. The command of a superior carries qualified immunity, but with a change in the degree of immunity as one ascends the ladder of authority. A platoon commander will instruct X to perform a certain action; but a colonel's instructions, and still more those of a general officer, will not be to an individual soldier but to a battalion, brigade or division. The instructions will be to aim at a certain objective using, if necessary, certain means; and the instructions will have to be broken down and particularised by the subordinate commanders. It follows that, while the principle of qualified liability applies to everyone under authority, the higher and more comprehensive the authority wielded, the more onerous will be the personal responsibility for decisions taken.

That general criminal liability tends to increase as we ascend the scale of command is a point of great practical importance with respect to such questions as the justification of arraigning and punishing for war crimes. There are many practical objections. It is the vanquished who are prosecuted. Do the tribunals have a genuine legal status or are the proceedings a form of lynch law? But practical difficulties should not obscure issues of principle. For high-ranking leaders liability will have at least two forms. There is the question of criminal liability with respect to the law of one's own State, and this is the more readily acknowledged. But the positive law of a State might well permit or order practices condemned as evil by sections of its own people or by other communities; and this is often the case under dictatorships. These are the conditions under which high-ranking officers of the State tend to claim unqualified immunity, the claim being based on the ground that the State is the highest earthly authority, and that crime is what the State declares it to be.

The flaw in this claim to unqualified immunity is that the positive law of the State is the most potent normative system within the moral order. It may be abysmally corrupt in many respects, but it is indispensible. The moral order therefore requires that if necessary, it should be reformed. It can be reformed only by the voluntary efforts of its members who are not only citizens of the State but also members of the moral order. Consequently, they can never claim immunity at the bar of moral judgement for acts committed in accordance with a system of positive law which is itself morally corrupt.

The general conclusion, then, is that, by the very nature of the social system which creates authorities empowered to order the commission of crimes, all persons under authority can bear only qualified liability, the degree of liability diminishing as one descends the hierarchy of command. But immunity can never be unqualified since there are always situations in which the conscience of even the most humble member of the moral order will be called on to adjudicate. We have discussed this topic in the extremely limited context of military service; but the general principles apply throughout the life of a community as a whole.

II. PUNISHMENT

We have assumed that the general aim of criminal law is to prevent wrongdoing; and to test the correctness of this assumption we have to consider two questions: (1) To whom is punishment applied? and (2) What is its apparent aim in actual practice?

(1) Liability to Punishment

When a wrong has been committed, it will have been consequential upon one or other of the following states of mind:[18]

(i) *Completely innocent mistake*, as when A, opening out a window-shutter, dislodges B who has been attempting a break-in and, through A's action, falls to his death. A did not know, nor is there any reason why he should have suspected that B was at the window. (ii) *Negligence*, as when a person unwittingly breaks the law, but would have known that he was breaking it had he been alert to the circumstances. (iii) *Recklessness*, as when a person, intent on an objective X, pursues it in the knowledge that certain unlawful consequences Y and Z may very well happen. Thus a person who, desiring to reach a destination in the shortest possible time, indulges in leap-frogging a traffic queue on a winding road, is acting recklessly. He desires to reach his destination, not to cause an accident, but he is aware that an accident may well result. (iv) *Intent*, as when a person sets himself directly and principally to the performance of an illegal action, e.g. an armed hold-up of a bank.

The two states of mind which, by universal practice, carry liability to punishment are (iii) and (iv). These evince an attitude of deliberate contempt for the law. With respect to (ii) practice varies because it is not easy to draw a sharp line between negligence and recklessness. The attitude of negligence is largely a matter of inference from the objective circumstances and gravity of the consequences. There are situations in which the serious dangers are so obvious to a reasonably lawabiding person that the negligence must have been gross, approaching to recklessness. When the culpability is only moderate it is not likely to be penalised since it does not imply disrespect for the law. It is, however, censurable as lacking the dedication which is a mark of good citizenship. (i) Completely innocent mistake is a clear defence to any charge, subject to the qualification that certain breaches of the law carry absolute liability. On 'absolute liability' there are differences of opinion. Some hold it to be an irrational departure from principle; others regard it as justified on grounds of sheer expediency. For our purposes, the important thing is that there is acknowledged to be a principle with regard to which this liability is admitted to be an exception. The principle is that the imposition of penalties is reasonable only in so far as prior knowledge of possible or certain illegal consequences of a proposed action do not deter from commiting it.

(2) Aim of Punishment

'Punishment' is a somewhat unsatisfactory term to cover the various forms of treatment meted out to convicted persons or to persons who, having committed a *prima facie* criminal act, are not considered fit subjects for punishment in the ordinary sense. As we are dealing only with those who are morally and legally responsible the two forms of treatment most relevant to our enquiry are the imposition of penalties as future deterrents and schemes of reformation. But the concept of retribution has a prominent place in theories of punishment, and so we shall begin with it.[19]

(1) Retribution

The *OED* gives: Retribution (from re + *tribuere*, to give, assign)—
1. Repayment, recompense, return for some service, merit, etc.
2. Day of Retribution, the day on which divine reward or punishment will be assigned to men.
3. A recompense for or requital of evil done.

Although the term is now used exclusively in sense 3, the earlier comprehensive use gives the clue to its essential meaning. Retribution is an act denoting approval or disapproval. If a soldier risks his life to rescue a wounded comrade, the act of retribution will probably be the award of the MM. If he deserts in face of the enemy the act of retribution will be (or used to be) the firing-squad. The award of the MM is the acknowledgement of behaviour highly approved, but it has in itself no ulterior purpose so far as that soldier is concerned, although it publishes to soldiers generally how such behaviour is regarded. Execution by a firing-squad is an intimation of high disapproval of the behaviour in question, but it has no ulterior purpose so far as that soldier is concerned, although the disapproval will be noted by others.

Retribution in the present narrow sense may amount to no more than spontaneous retaliation, as e.g. impulsive blow for unexpected blow. At that simple level it cannot be said to have any aim, not even the aim of shewing disapproval, since it is not a voluntary action (as explained above).

But when it is practised under a rule—the *lex talionis*, eye for eye, tooth for tooth—it is a voluntary action. As such, it is purposive, having some end in view, however obscurely. This is true even of the blood-feud, each killing being required to sustain the family honour. On much the same level, though in a more complex form, was the ancient punishment meted out to the builder whose client's house collapsed, killing his son. The builder's own house was deliberately demolished with his son inside. As the punishment was, so far as possible, an exact replica of the crime, its imposition must have been motivated by an idea of 'balancing down', the inverted image of the 'balancing up' which takes place in reparation. Retribution here precedes the stage at which we make a clear distinction between the physical act (*actus reus*) and the mental attitude (*mens rea*), or the distinction between reparation and punishment.

However, the first of these distinctions is implicit in the ancient Jewish allocation of different penalties to two acts of manslaughter,[20] one of which occurred in the heat of sudden confrontation and the other by way of ambush. Here the penalty is clearly directed to the attitude of will; and as this becomes increasingly recognised to be the appropriate target for punishment, so punishment no longer aims at 'fitting the crime' in the sense of balancing down by reproducing the criminal act. It is conceived as a means to an end, notifying the consequences which will follow the wrongful act, hoping that the prospective wrongdoer will abandon his purpose.

It is thus evident that, while retribution at its simplest level can be nothing more than involuntary retaliation, an act of disapproval, once it is deliberately adopted and institutionalised the disapproval is expressed in the form of a penal sanction with a deterrent purpose.

(2) Deterrence

Some moral and legal theorists seem to regard retribution as one of the *aims* of punishment. This is a mistake. Retribution *is* punishment, its aim being to deter the prospective criminal by published threat. Reluctance to regard deterrence as the sole aim seems to be associated with the idea that this purely utilitarian motive would justify morally indefensible practices. It is said that, since the method of deterrence consists in publishing and carrying out threats, the desired result could on occasion be achieved by punishing an innocent man who appeared to be guilty. The failure to punish him would suggest that crime can be committed with impunity.

It is rather difficult to see just what is meant by 'the innocent who appears to be guilty'. We know that a person who is in fact innocent may be declared guilty and punished; but this is not conscious punishment of the innocent; it is a case of mistake of fact. Even those who say 'When in doubt, convict; for it is better that an innocent man should suffer than that the guilty should go free' are not subscribing to the view that the innocent should be punished. At most, they are saying only 'We should presume guilt if the evidence is evenly balanced, and abandon the safeguard of requiring 'proof beyond reasonable doubt'. Again, it is true that in order to impress public opinion with their efficiency, or for some other reason, some policemen will suppress or plant evidence to secure a conviction; but punishment will not follow unless the charge is believed by the court to be true.

'Punishing the innocent' must mean something different from any of these examples. What the argument is maintaining is that, if deterrence is the sole aim of the infliction of penalties, the administration of justice can be advanced by corrupting justice at its source, namely in the court of law. It makes no sense to talk of punishing 'the innocent' unless we mean '*known* to be innocent by the judge imposing the sentence'. How would he know? Was he told that the jury really meant 'not guilty' when they said 'guilty'? Or was he privy to a compact between prosecution and defence to distort the evidence placed before the jury? The postulate is that somehow he knew the man to be innocent while treating him as guilty. But the more one tries to understand the implications—the idea of deterring crime in general by the corruption of justice in particular, punishing the innocent *pour encourager les autres*—the more does one realise that this is one of those cloud-cuckoos apt to be flushed by the beaters in a philosophical shoot.

Returning to the *terra firma* of commonsense, we note that punishment intended as a deterrent assumes voluntary conduct to be as we have ourselves described it. The threat of a penalty is expected to have a deterrent influence because it is an appeal to the potential wrongdoer's reason. His intention to commit a crime is a valuation, a potential choice to adopt the course of action 'required' by his scheme of values and his assessment of the factual situation. If we wish to prevent his acting in that way, then, short of imposing physical restraint, we have to do it by confronting him with an adjusted set of circumstances. The adjustment consists in attaching new consequences to the action, consequences which will be detrimental to some element in his existing scheme of values, the hope being that, on reflection, he will decide to abstain. The appeal is throughout an appeal to his reason. The original intention, to commit the crime, was a rational response to an existing system of ends and the assessment of an existing external situation. The abandonment of the project in order to retain that system of ends in a changed external situation would be equally rational. We are, of course, talking of the hopes of the lawmaker. If the adjustment does not meet the case, the situation will be further modified.

The threat and use of penalties has a further point of interest in connexion with our account of voluntary conduct. We saw that, when attempting to overcome an addiction, a person will make use of aids to assist the resolution. Filters, pills, rigorous regimes at special clinics, etc., are used to counter the physiological and psychological conditions to which the craving is a response. The deliberate alteration of conditions is intended to create a situation the assessment of which will 'require' a choice other than a surrender to the craving. The threat of penalties is a corresponding arrangement of circumstances to influence the choice away from the contemplated criminal act. In the one case we have a set of aids adopted by the agent himself. In the other case we have a set of 'aids' (threatened penalties) imposed on him by an outside authority.

When we make this comparison, it reminds us that the aids adopted by a person to overcome an addiction can be permanently successful only as buttresses to a firm resolution to succeed. The same must be true of sanctions intended to deter from crime. Of themselves they appeal to reason, but not to reason under the form of Universality. The appeal is to a person's sense of

Economy, inviting him to consider the value of the end to be attained by the crime relatively to some other end or ends which will be forfeited. The success of this appeal can be limited for two reasons. First, the potential wrongdoer may not passively accept the new situation. He may initiate counter-adjustments; and the more highly intelligent he is, the greater will be his chance of playing the game with success—avoiding detection, finding loopholes in the law, corrupting its officers. Secondly, no penalty is directed against wrongdoing in general. Penalties are specific, aimed at specific types of behaviour. Hence, even when most effective, the penalty, as such, can deter only from its type of wrongdoing. Of course we have to bear in mind that a term of imprisonment will have complex effects. We have also to remember that a sharp punishment for a particular misdemeanour may jolt a first offender into a sense of his social responsibilities. But that is not the aim of a specific penalty. It does not of itself tend to increase respect for law in general. It is a particular appeal to enligh: · ·d self-interest.

(3) Reformation

It is precisely an appeal to reason under the concept of Universality that is attempted in reformative treatment. And such treatment is indeed encouraged by the very assumptions made in the use of penal sanctions. Their imposition assumes that the wrongdoer is a rational being in the fullest sense, capable of being governed by the supreme form of Practical Reason namely Universality. This is implied by the fact that the penalty is imposed for *culpable* behaviour. The culpability does not consist in having acted against enlightened self-interest. The infliction of the penalty assumes that the person has been motivated by what he deemed to be his interest, and it is appealing to precisely the same motive to produce conformity in an altered situation. Yet, in regarding the action as having been culpable, we are implying that he was fully *capable* of conforming from the higher motive.

This analysis of the thinking behind the practice of deterrent punishment enables us to draw a conclusion of the greatest practical importance, namely that anyone to whom such punishment can properly be applied is, on that very ground, capable by nature of responding to reformative treatment. The capability is implied because fully rational nature is implied. This conclusion does not tell us what treatment would be effective; nor does it forecast the chances of success in individual cases. It merely indicates the capability as a necessary attribute of rational nature. Nonetheless, the general truth of the analysis seems to be confirmed by present trends in our own and other democratic countries, trends which place increasing emphasis on the idea of reformation.

It should be added that reformative treatment also presupposes our analysis of the nature of voluntary conduct. A large part of the treatment consists in making adjustments to the external circumstances of the past, and potentially future, wrongdoer. In these adjustments, however, the threat of penalty plays a minor part. Some factors in a person's existing environment actually encourage crime and delinquency, and much of the reformative treatment is necessarily devoted to creating conditions conducive to the development of a sense of social responsibility, to educating the will in the adoption of legal and moral standards as its own.

(4) Elimination

There is a radical difference between the imposition of deterrent sanctions and reformative treatment, on the one hand, and the infliction of capital punishment, on the other. The former presume the possibility of the criminal's survival to become a loyal member of the community, while the latter secures the termination of his criminal activities by terminating his existence. And yet, the person on whom capital punishment is inflicted is also assumed to be a potentially loyal member of the community. He is being punished; punishment assumes culpability; culpability implies the potentiality of acting as a member of the moral order.

Is there, then, any moral justification for the inclusion of capital punishment within the criminal law of a civilised State? To this question two answers representing opposite extremes have been given.

First, Kant once affirmed that, if a society were about to dissolve, one of its final measures should be to execute the last remaining murderer. This view, presumably, regards every wrongful act as meriting its appropriate punishment; and it seems to be making an appeal to the *lex talionis*—eye for eye, tooth for tooth, life for life. This is certainly not an attitude characteristic of civilised society. Execution for murder gives the required correspondence for 'the punishment to fit the crime'. But in the course of our history this punishment has also been imposed for treason, piracy, adultery, sheep stealing, coining and heresay; and it is impossible to see its fittingness in any of these cases. For example, would not the proper punishment for adultery, according to the *lex talionis*, be for the spouses of the guilty pair to commit adultery with each other?

At the other extreme is the contention that capital punishment is utterly incompatible with the moral order since it violates the sanctity of personality which has absolute value. There is here a confusion between the idea of a person as the *source* of values and the idea of his having *absolute value*. There are, in fact, no absolute values. The value of anything is always relative to other values in the system to which it belongs. Should it be replied that the argument against capital punishment is even stronger if personality is the source of all values, this is countered by the explanation that a person is the source of all values which can be values to *him*. His value systems do not determine the value systems of other persons. There may be valid reasons for excluding capital punishment from the moral order; but there is no ground for supposing that this exclusion is a basic assumption of the law of civilised society.

If we look at the considerations which do in fact influence public opinion and criminal law, these fall well within the two extremes.

Thus, for the retention or re-introduction of capital punishment, there does not seem to be particularly widespread feeling against the man who shoots his wife and her lover or against the distraught woman who has killed her child. Resentment is directed against armed robbery, kidnapping for ransom; and it is particularly strong against the fact that a person venturing on the street in certain localities risks being set upon, robbed and kicked or stabbed to death. These it is said, are cancers which must be cut from the body politic.

For the abolition of capital punishment, one argument concerns the character it imposes on criminal procedure. Perhaps most people concede that, if necessary, the State is justified in using armed police to deal with armed terrorists. This is a preventive measure taken in a present emergency. But there is a considerable degree of revulsion against the long drawn out court procedure which can only take place after the event. The reaction need not be on the ground that the procedure is unjust. Indeed the ritual is long drawn out and formal to ensure, if possible, that injustice may not be done. The reaction is against the fact that such procedure is necessary to secure conviction and punishment. It is felt that, in the interests of humanity for many of the people concerned, the penalty should be foregone rather than imposed at such a price.

These are just two of the arguments which may be advanced for and against capital punishment; but they do not touch the question of principle, the question of moral justification.

Moral justification is a matter for Conscience, the conscience of the individual passing judgement on what is required by the moral order; and its decisions are authoritative for that individual, and for him alone. Hence, if we are to consider the moral justification of State action, it must be on some principle derived analogically from the sphere of individual morality.

Looking, then, at the matter in its individual context, suppose that we ask whether it can be morally justifiable to take the life of another person, conscience does not reply to this question in general terms. It delivers judgement only in a specific situation where the taking of life is proposed as a means to some specific end. As we have seen in Chapter VIII (pp. 60ff), a judgment of moral right or wrong is concerned with the question whether a person is able to universalise the maxim of his proposed action. With regard to taking life, the really crucial issue will be whether it is justifiable to kill in self-defence. Let us say that A is a Roman Catholic (Protestant) who refuses (gives) allegiance to the present government of Northern Ireland, and that B decides to kill him on that account. Is A entitled to resist even to the point of killing B in self-defence? Of course there might well be other ways of effective resistance; but the question is whether, as a last resort, killing B could be morally justified. Could A universalise his maxim: 'I propose in these circumstances to kill B in order to prevent his killing me'? Could he accept that every person in precisely his situation would be entitled to take that means to that end? If he could so universalise his maxim, then he would be morally entitled to act on it.

It must be noted that the universalisation of a maxim does not prescribe a person's moral *duty*. It proclaims a moral *right*; and moral rights, like other rights, can be waived and not exercised. Thus if someone has the moral right to kill in self-defence, he may nonetheless feel obliged to offer no resistance on religious or some other ideal ground. This duty of non-resistance is not of a higher order than his moral right. It is a duty to which he feels committed within the bounds of his moral right.

If self-defence is assumed to be the only ground on which the private individual may take another's life, it follows that, in looking for a social analogy, we must begin by identifying a corresponding threat to society. Perhaps the nearest equivalent would be the attempt to impede the essential functions of a government enjoying the confidence of the community in general. Such attacks are in fact made in some well established democracies by terrorist groups, their methods being the assassination of key figures in the Executive and Judiciary. The question, then, will be whether the State has the moral right to eliminate such persons by the inclusion of capital punishment within its system of criminal law. The answer is surely that anyone who accords to the private individual the right to ward off death or serious bodily injury by killing the aggressor must grant the right of capital punishment to the State.

But again, we must note that this is a moral right, not a moral duty. It will be within the discretion of the State to decide if it will exercise this right, and if so under what conditions.

This is as far as the moral philosopher can go in dealing with the issue of capital punishment. He can elucidate the principles of the moral order; but their detailed interpretation and application are matters for the private individual and State government.

Appendix

ON THE NECESSARY CONNEXION BETWEEN LAW AND MORALITY

The standpoint adopted in this book has been that, while the essential structure of a moral order derives ultimately from practical reason as operative in the Conscience of the moral agent, the operation of Conscience in moral judgement can be understood only with the assistance of legal theory in which we find a systematic exposition of the basic concepts common to law and morals.

This puts the relationship of law and morals from the point of view of the moralist. But that relationship is also of concern to the legal theorist; and it is natural to ask whether ethics is as important for jurisprudence as jurisprudence is for ethics. Is there, in short, a 'necessary connexion' between law and morality? The matter has been extensively debated in the history of jurisprudence, many of the issues being beyond the competence of the layman to discuss. We may, however, take the question on a broad basis, starting with what seems to be an assertion of complete independence.

There is a tendency for the layman to confuse questions of postive law with those of morals; and so the lawyer is tempted to insist on the distinction in ways which obscure the relationship. Thus, in the opening paragraph of Sheriff Gordon's account of legal responsibility (*Criminal Law,* p. 45), though certainly not in the substantial account itself, the distinction is presented as a separation. He begins by saying that legal responsibility is *a*moral, illustrating the point by the example of a teacher who, before leaving the class-room, singles out one of the boys and says 'I shall hold you responsible for any noise there may be in my absence'. Responsibility is here imputed without reference to the boy's power to prevent the noise. However morally reprehensible such an attitude may be (the argument continues), there is nothing inherently illogical in saying to someone 'I know you are in no way to blame for this situation, but I am going to hold you responsible for it' (nothing illogical in saying 'I say you are not responsible but say you are responsible '?); and such an expression of intention to hold someone responsible is, in the last resort, the basis of legal responsibility.

The implication is that the imputation of responsibility is an arbitrary fiat; and the fictitious example of the teacher's order may be thought to have a real parallel in an incident told of Captain Packer RN (*Deep As The Sea,* by Joy Packer). Passing along the dockside, he came on some ratings engaged on a fatigue. Having noted his approach, they continued with their work. He stopped and asked 'Who is in charge here?'. Apparently no one. 'Who is the longest serving rating?'. An individual having identified himself, Packer asked 'Why did you not call the party to attention and salute as I passed?'. Following the reprimand, he explained: for the navy, discipline is absolutely essential at all times and in all circumstances; and there is always someone responsible for its enforcement—if no petty-officer present, the senior able seaman; if no able seaman, the longest serving ordinary seaman.

This, of course, is not a real parallel to the teacher's fiat; and the difference is brought out with the elaboration of Sheriff Gordon's own argument: 'The rules of a school may say that . . . the senior boy present will be held responsible, and the rules of an army may say that a particular officer is responsible for the cleanliness of a particular barrack-room'. 'Senior boy' and 'officer' are responsible within a normative order which accords to them a status, an authority backed by the rules which give them power. The exposition then continues (p.47), shewing that responsibility under the criminal law does in fact rest almost entirely on moral ideas of praise and blame.

But is this a merely factual relationship? The idea that it is a necessary one is considered in great detail by Hart in *The Concept of Law* where 'morality' refers, not to the individual judgement (as in this book) but to the content of a social consensus. This is a perfectly legitimate and very common meaning of the term, but it poses the 'law-morality' relationship in a way different from that in which it has been dealt with in the foregoing chapters. That being understood, the substance of Hart's view may be put in the following way:

(p.168) Law and morality have a common vocabulary in the use of terms such as law, right, duty, obligation; and that this is no accident is shewn by the similarity of legal and moral rules and their authoritative character. As expressing a social consensus, they are binding independently of individual consent; they are supported by social pressures which may be as effective as legal sanctions to secure conformity; they prohibit violence to person or property; they demand honesty and truthfulness in inter-personal relations. (pp.169ff) There are, however, characteristics which law and morality do not share, and morality has four cardinal distinctive features. First, while rules of law may prescribe acts or forbearances which no one (now) considers important, this is never true of moral rules which cease to be authoritative when they cease to be considered important. Second, since moral rules do not originate in formal enactment, they cannot be deliberately changed. They develop, remain in force, and decay by consensus. Third, moral innocence and culpability are measured by the mental attitude of a person when choosing to act; and this is not wholly true in positive law which recognises areas of 'strict liability'. Fourth, the sanctions—the forms of pressure to induce conformity—are not the same.

If, then, we ask whether there is a necessary relation between law and morality, Hart's answer would seem to be something like this: There is such a relationship because of the nature of man—a roughly natural equality to help or harm, a natural desire to continue existing and to have a share in the same means of survival. No system of law can be an effective ('good') system which does not meet these natural requirements, distributing opportunities in a just, equitable manner.

But the fact that a system of law is effective only so far as it meets natural demands, and that it can meet the demands of members of a group only by paying regard to principles of justice so far as they are embodied in the social consensus, does not mean that there is a necessary relationship between the *concept* of law and the *concept* of morality. Such a necessary relationship would mean that law by definition would include a reference to morality. It would mean that no rule could be accepted as a rule of law if it could truly be described as unjust. This would be contrary to all experience and commonsense.

This is true; but it is not the whole truth. If by 'morality' we mean the content of a social consensus persisting alongside of, and to some extent overlapping that of the legal order, then it is true that the only 'necessary' connexion between the law and the morality of a given community is a reflection of the natural constitution and survival needs of its members. They demand that the content of the law be adjusted to the satisfaction of those needs. This is the level at which party policies are presented to the public at a general election.

But there is a different point of view from which law and morality can be seen to be necessarily related in an unqualified sense. This is the relationship between the judicial process and personal moral judgement. It is a relationship based, not on the expressed needs of the members of a community but on the nature of a moral order which determines the decisions as to how those needs are to be met. This was not Hart's theme, but the point is implicit in parts of his argument: a legal judgement is a judgement in accordance with a rule recognised by the judge; and judgment according to rule involves treating like cases alike and unlike cases differently.

What is here stated in general principle is made explicit in Professor Neil MacCormick's *Legal Reasoning and Legal Theory* (Clarendon Law Series: Oxford 1978), one purpose of which is to shew the nature of legal argumentation characteristic of litigation and adjudication upon disputed matters of law. The work of a thoroughly professional jurist, the book is also an important contribution to ethics, and two chapters are especially relevant to the Kantial analysis of moral judgement.

The Kantian test of the moral quality of a proposed action is the universalisability of its maxim, and MacCormick's chapter on 'The Constraint of Formal Justice' (IV) assigns to the concept of Universality the same status in legal judgement. This is brought out in pp. 77ff and in the concluding paragraph (.99):

The thesis here argued is a clear and straightforward one. It is that the notion of formal justice requires that the justification of decisions in individual cases be always on the basis of universal propositions to which the judge is prepared to adhere as a basis for determining other like cases and deciding them in the like manner to the present one.

The essential kindred of legal and moral judgement is not weakened by the fact that in the judicial process the judge must 'find' explicitly or implicitly contained in the existing body of law the universal validating his judgement, while in morals the agent must autonomously will the universal giving validity to his action.

In Chapter V, 'Second Order Justification', MacCormick stresses the fact that in many instances a court is faced by two or more possible universals, and he shews (pp. 103ff) that the choice between them is governed by the requirement that legal decision should 'make sense in the real world'; and making sense is largely concerned with the conditions of a reasonably happy life in organised society.

As to the relationship with Kantian ethics, MacCormick accepts that judicial reasoning and the Kantian account of moral judgement are at one in stressing the notion of universalisation; but (p. 123) he thinks that Kant's ethics fails to 'make sense in the real world' because of the complete autonomy ascribed to the will as pure practical reason. This criticism is amply justified by much, not only in the *Critique of Practical Reason* but also in the *Groundwork* itself, where practical reason is set in sheer opposition to our desiring nature as the source of 'heteronomy'. Were these passages to be taken, as they very often are, as representing the essential Kant, his analysis of moral judgement would be wholly at variance with what he professed to be doing, namely elucidating the moral thinking of ordinary people. But philosophers have never been able to ignore him because of a different range of ideas, starting with the initial locus of moral assessment, and passing through the formulation of principles to the conception of the Kingdom-of-Ends. There is an inner logic in this progression, forcing its way through the obscurantist relics of his early Rationalism; and it is this inner logic which I have tried to follow in Chapter VIII. It presents us with a theory of moral reasoning which certainly makes sense in the real world. The clue to the practical relevance is in his conception of a 'maxim'. Beginning with a down-to-earth desire for some end in certain circumstances and requiring certain means for its realisation, a person will make explicit the maxim he proposes to follow—I shall pursue this end x by these means y in these circumstances z. The moral question arises when he asks whether he could universalise the maxim, affirming the right or duty of every person everywhere to pursue such an end by such means in such circumstances. Could he will that in this instance all like cases should be treated alike? This is analogous to the issue placed before a judge. The moral agent (like the judge), having been bred in the ethos of a certain society, and now faced by an issue directly involved with day-to-day values, employs the same test of universalisability as that applied by the judge to any rule proposed to him as the basis of a decision.

In short, the real meaning of autonomy in Kantian ethics is not (as he so frequently suggests) the capacity of a rational will to take decisions uninfluenced by mundane values and traditional norms; it is the capacity to take responsibility for a final decision, those values and norms having been taken into account. This is the autonomy intrinsic to the judicial office; and that is why a work on 'legal reasoning' can be so illuminating for the student of ethics.

References

PART ONE

p3. 1) G E Moore, *Principia Ethica*, I 5-17; III 50; VI 112. See also W D Lamont, *Principles of Moral Judgement*, APPENDIX

p7. 2) Metrical Paraphrase of *Proverbs* III 13-17

p14. 3) Quoted in A Lane Poole, *Domesday Book to Magna Carta*, p. 52

p17. 4) Hastings Rashdall, *The Theory of Good and Evil*

p18. 5) J C Smuts, *Jan Christian Smuts*

p18. 6) Janet Adam Smith, *John Buchan*

p25. 7) W W Buckland, *Textbook of Roman Law*, p. 173

p25. 8) R H Thouless, *General and Social Psychology*, CH.X

p26. 9) R H Thouless, *General and Social Psychology*, CH. XIV, p. 252

p29. 10) W D Ross, *Foundations of Ethics*, CH.X

p29. 11) C A Campbell, *In Defence of Free Will*, PART I, Philosophy of Morals; and W G MacLagan, *The Theological Frontier of Ethics*

p30. 12) Kant, *Critique of Pure Reason*, trans. N K Smith. Pages 30-31 above shew the type of argument by which Kant established the *a priori* postulates of ordinary experience. The argument actually used with respect to the *a priori* postulate of causality was based on the distinction between a series of perceptions with irreversible contents and a series with reversible contents; but it is so tortuous and uneven that anyone wishing to pursue the subject should begin with Dr A C Ewing's *Kant's Treatment of Causality*.

PART TWO

p44. 1) *Genesis* XV 7-12 & 17-18: Peake's *Commentary on the Bible* (1967) 'The Covenant Ritual', pp. 190-191

p47. 2) Buckland, *op. cit.* pp. 58f

p47. 3) F M Stenton, *Anglo-Saxon England*, CH.IX; A G Richey, *Short History of the Irish People*, CH. III; F Seebohm, *Tribal Custom in Anglo-Saxon Law*, CH. II; W F Skene, *Celtic Scotland*, VOL. III

p48. 4) The Structure of the 'Fine' is indicated in passages scattered throughout the volumes of *The Ancient Laws of Ireland*, but the general character is described in Skene, *op. cit.* VOL. III, CH. V, and in Gearoid Mac Niocaill, *Ireland Before the Vikings*, CH. III

p48. 5) Stair, *Institutions of the Laws of Scotland*, I i 22, and quoted in T B Smith, *Short Commentary on the Law of Scotland*, p. 279

p49. 6) Gloag and Henderson, *Introduction to the Law of Scotland*, CH. III; T B Smith, *op. cit.* CH. 9

p55. 7) Translated by H J Paton under the title *The Moral Law* (Hutchinson's University Library)

p60. 8) Forms of 'the golden rule'—LEVITICUS XIX, 18; DEUTERONOMY VI, 5; MATT. XXII. 35-40; MK. XII, 28-34; LK. X, 25-28